THE
WAY
OUT

THE
WAY
OUT

by Mme Jeanne Guyon

CHRISTIAN BOOKS
GARDINER, MAINE

CHRISTIAN BOOKS
PUBLISHING HOUSE
Box 959
Gardiner, Maine 04345

ACKNOWLEDGEMENT

For nearly 100 years this book — Exodus — has been out of print, appearing in English only once, just previous to the beginning of the twentieth century. Rather than reprint that old edition we decided to modernize Mme. Guyon's commentary on Exodus and bring out a whole new edition in clear, modern English. The painstaking task was done by Ann Witkower of California. All of us who read and enjoy this wholly "new" book owe her a great debt.

1

God has given to you, throughout church history, many examples of individuals who have lived out their lives abandoned to Him. But He has also given you an example of an entire people, a nation, so that all generations to come may have a visible example of *how* to travel that selfsame road of abandonment. And for *you*, if you are called into this internal walk, *you* must know that you must walk through this same captivity and through all the reverses that this people experienced.

Was there any nation more prosperous than this people when Joseph was alive? All the best things in the kingdom were in their hand. Yet we see this nation was brought into captivity. Is a believer different from Judah? No. Every believer who dares to walk the spiritual way will have ineffable joy; *but* there will also be another favor God will give you. He has assured it to all those of His children who are faithful to Him:

He makes them to undergo captivity.

Jesus Christ was the first to enter into this experience. He was the Chief of all those abandoned ones, yet He was not exempt from this *captivity.* Therefore it is impossible that *you* will be exempt. Always remember, it pleased Him to come forth from all the delights that were hidden in His Father's bosom, to become the most captive of all men.

Remember, too, that long ago the Hebrew Patriarchs followed this same path. Joy, delight . . . *and* captivity! The early believers of the new covenant came along and they followed in the order of the Patriarchs *and* their divine model, Jesus Christ.

But you will ask, "Why must we all pass this way? Is it so that we can all be made unhappy?" Of course not. Joy is promised in the land of Abraham . . . a land which lies out there *beyond* captivity. What is that land? That land is . . . possessing *God*! But, oh, how much must *be done* to possess that land. There is suffering to be known!

Look at Pharaoh. God used this man to cause God's faithful Hebrews to enter into captivity. Nor is Pharaoh the only one whom your Lord employs. Pharaoh also has *taskmasters*! Together these Egyptians overwhelmed God's people in *labor*, thinking they would oppress this people and prevent them from becoming greater in number. (Beware of too much "Christian" labor.)

2

The same is true today. Throughout history there has arisen some strong power or authority that decides it must extinguish the *interior* walk. They use persecution, they use shouts, denunciations and everything in their hands. Ah, but it is then that the interior life *most* multiplies. And what is the result? The more these powers teach against such a walk, and persecute it, the more people are found joining the ranks of those who pursue this path. It is persecution that establishes and increases people of the interior way.

The powers of darkness join in to overwhelm you and increase your burden beyond bearing. But the more the soul is laden, the more weakness experienced, the more there rises up inside, like a palm tree, something of God within. *And* this life multiplies itself.

The hardest persecution for God's people to bear is to see their lives wasted laboring for the things of this world, knowing all the time that they are called to the table of God. Such believers know that the work on this earth produces nothing at all. Yet here they are! They have become wholly earthly, themselves.

At this time the followers of an internal walk are laughed at by their enemies. The Egyptians watched God's people being forced to turn away from the things they loved, to the building of cities for the Egyptians.

Persecution went beyond hate and enslavement. The Egyptians next sought to destroy the birth from these people. Unfortunately even in the world of what is supposed to be true religion, men — considered enlightened — work very hard to get the beginning Christian to turn from the interior way. They are men who are like kings. They are appointed of God to be shepherds of our souls, yet they oppose that very soul. They oppose the believer doing those things which would bring him into the greatest fellowship with God. And those religious leaders who do not condemn this walk, also do not sanction it. In so doing they keep as many — or more — people from truths and from light. The beginners, so in need of this light, are prevented from drawing close to Jesus Christ.

Such obstructive men neither enter the Kingdom, nor do they allow others to go in.

Please notice that it is the 'male child' which Egypt is after. This signifies the courageous believer (be that believer male *or* female), one who is willing to be abandoned. As you live out your life, you will see men about you who are quite willing to let those around them live in peace . . . *if* those people are living in a *com-*

4

promised love toward the Lord! In fact, such leaders enjoy being with such ones, and like to have them living their lives out around them. But to those who are wholly committed to Him, and to an internal walk, such Egyptians do not wish to see *these* people prosper! They would be more pleased if such people did not exist.

Men cannot bear such love and such a walk. But as destruction of God's people looms, something encouraging happens. The command has gone out to stamp out a love of God, but a few in the Egyptian world are gained over to this happy state. They present their energies to *preserve* the heavenly walk. He, or she, has been won over because of having a simple *heart*. Rarely is this seen among the more complex, gifted and wise, especially if they are also religious.

It is the simple *midwives* who prevent the destruction of God's most special people.

And those simple midwives who protected His children "were established in their houses." Recompense and reward is given by the Spirit of God to those who have protected the ones whom He has called.

Persecution was not enough, enslavement was not enough; death was the final desire of God's enemy. Pharaoh has ordered all the male children to be cast into the river. To those who dare to be wholly His, be sure *these* people are either cast into the river or exposed to extreme dangers. From whence comes these dangers?

From temptations! From being forced to follow in the way of the world! From distrust and fear, brought in among God's people — as a result His most precious followers are scattered, or perish.

Sometimes there is no more than the destruction of one's reputation. These are all extreme dangers. Such "rivers" await *you*.

As you live out your life upon this earth, you will notice that only the "manchild" is touched. No others are cast out, nor persecuted, nor are they threatened with the river. These people are secure. Their *shallow* walk guarantees that they will be secure! Persecution and slander are rarely their lot.

On the contrary, sometimes you will find these ones are *elevated*, in order to ruin others.

2

What does the birth and rescue of Moses show us?

The one who would lead the people of Providence is born a child of Providence! You can be sure that a child who was exposed to the impetuosity of severe ways, will rise one day to be a shepherd of God's people. That his mother hides him from death is, of course, a striking figure of Jesus Christ. We must remember that the Lord's nativity, as Savior of the world, follows the example of Moses.

Let us look at the mother of Moses.

She confronts superior forces. Her intellect says 'yield,' but she prefers to trust God alone. She *relinquishes* her child and exposes him to the waters, knowing not whether those waters will be merciful or otherwise. It is only *in extreme peril* that you can understand true abandonment; and it is in those moments that God chooses, most frequently, to show His goodness and His providence. And it is sometimes in *extreme peril* he shows forth unheard of miracles!

Watch as Moses is cast into the river. Will he

be carried off by the waves? What can be hoped for this child? Death? A watery burial? Certainly death seems inevitable. The little boat he is in is nothing but a living coffin. Yet it is from this coffin of death that God draws him.

Here is a man who has been in the providence of God from his cradle; a cradle that was supposed to be his tomb. Shall we say the cradle is his coffin? Or shall we say that the coffin was his cradle? Perhaps the second is more true, for — from the beginning of his life — he had to go through the extreme passageways of God's providence, and live out his life in the dangers of death.

It is interesting to note that at the very moment Moses is placed in the waters, Pharaoh's daughter came to the river. In the ways of God, those who condemn us to death are sometimes those who save our lives.

It would be a small event in the ways of God if a child were born to the providence of God and then abandoned. But that providence in his life will continue all the days of his life.

You can see this very truth in the fact that Pharaoh chooses Moses' own mother to be his nurse, though Pharaoh knows nothing of their kinship!

What a Lord have we! Why not then trust Him?

Please note, now, that Moses grows up in the courts of this world. He knows the court's grandeur, he knows its dangers. As a grown man he must choose either to live in this life of "Egypt," or turn away from it. Outwardly he looks like an Egyptian, and he is considered the son of the Princess. But in his heart he is a Hebrew. There is more treasure in this man than appears, for the treasures are hidden within.

Paul said, "The true Jew is not one outwardly, but one inwardly. True circumcision is not outward, it is of the heart and of the Spirit. It is not of the letter."

Here again you can see Moses as a figure of Christ. Outwardly he appeared to be simply a man, yet inwardly there was something of the true God. Jesus Christ *resembled* the sinners, but He was the Holy of Holies.

There is a lesson here: We are not judged by outward appearance. It is what is going on *in the depths* of a man that decides his course and destiny.

But can a man who is a prince in Pharaoh's court find *a way out*?

We see Moses losing his place in the house of

Pharaoh! But why? By what means? Essentially it is because of his shepherd's heart. He is there taking care of one of the Lord's own people. There is faithfulness in this man; there is care for the flock of God. Be careful. A true concern for the lot of God's spiritual people can bring you great trouble. Even disenfranchisement!

Moses is cast out *into the wilderness*. He is out of Egypt, but immediately he is in the wilderness!

Once more the defense of truth has been followed by persecution coming from the hands of avowed enemies. This is *not* an exception. None who come after him will be excepted, either.

We now see Moses fleeing. He is taking part in the life of the interior believer. He is being persecuted for righteousness' sake. But is there more to it than that? Moses now becomes a shepherd of a little flock in a wilderness. We are told this is God's divine design for Moses. What is Moses doing there in the wilderness?

He is watering the flock.

Moses is not a shepherd of one particular group, he is the shepherd of all the sheep. He has defended the sheep and now he is watering them. All true shepherds who follow in the example of Jesus Christ are such. They give water, they defend those who are the Lord's . . . against His enemies. They make sure that the water is there, freely to be drunk even though their enemy would hinder the drinking.

There were unjust shepherds there in the wilderness who were trying to prevent those sheep from being watered. But the water is given to them by Moses the shepherd. You may expect, if you are one abandoned to Him, that the Lord may send a Moses into your life to give you water in the wilderness and to deliver you from oppression and from ignorant shepherds who *hinder* sheep from *reaching* water.

Abandoned ones, no matter what they have suffered, will eventually *find* water *if* they are faithful.

Abandoned ones will discover the faithfulness of God. He will send someone to them who will instruct them in the ways of the Lord.

You will notice that the women who were rescued by Moses out in the wilderness returned to their father to report to him what had happened to them. There you see what each of us must do: that is, to return to our source, our Father. The good Shepherd has given us pure water and caused us to advance toward our Father.

It is now that the will of God becomes so clear. The father of those whom Moses aided has invited Moses to his very home. There Moses finds the companionship of Zipporah, one who will share with Moses his calling and his faithfulness. With him she will make a contribution to that spiritual generation.

It was here, in this place, that Moses found retreat until the hour when he would lead God's people. *Such is the purpose of a true wilderness.*

And now we gain an insight into Zipporah, in the birth of her child. When she gave birth to a child, Eliezer, she immediately turned to the Lord and gave Him the praise by saying, "The God of my father is my protector and He has delivered me from the hand of Pharaoh."

When you see one of God's children attributing everything to the providence of God you see something of that person's heart. Reproduction, our children — our everything — comes from His hand. When we walk in the knowledge of that, we are signifying a true enlightenment toward God ... by a living faith, we are acknowledging that His ways are just and that from Him we receive our succor.

We come to the close of chapter two with a very powerful scene that teaches us much.

Moses is in the wilderness being raised up by God. *But the Lord's people,* back in Egypt, *do not know this!*

Pharaoh dies; perhaps at this time they expect deliverance, but no deliverance comes. Their groanings increase. They are overwhelmed and they raise their cries to heaven. But it seems the Lord does not hear. Is that true? He did hear! Even at that moment — unseen — He is answering. He *did* remember His covenant with Abraham! In due time He will show compassion upon them. You must remember that God has a covenant with you and that whatever happens to you upon this earth, *He has not forgotten that covenant.*

God's people in Egypt are telling us three things: they are people of faith, of total sacrifice, and of perfect abandonment.

Abraham is the father of *faith.* It was Isaac who was marked by the pure *sacrifice.* And Jacob, in his old age, was perfect *abandonment.* You, if you are to walk the interior way, will walk by three things: first, by a *faith* that is blind toward the *ways* of your God, that is by a faith wholly fixed on God . . . *regardless.* What do we mean by a *total* faith? Even *naked* faith? It is a faith which does not ask for a sign, and it is faith which does not seek support from reason, logic or any other sources which the mind of man can afford.

What is a total *sacrifice*? A *pure* sacrifice? Not only is it the laying down of all things which belong to us and all things which are in us, but *all that we are*. You lay down all, as far as grace has allowed you to lay down *all*.

And what is total and perfect abandonment? This is an estate of complete destitution in God's hand. We say to Him, "Lord, You may do all in me, whatever is wholly Your will. Your will can be worked out in me." But be careful. We speak here mostly of internal things: God working *within* you to bring you to full stature . . . doing this work throughout *time*, and working also even throughout *eternity*.

Remember that. There may be no sign of it, but He is faithful. He has not forgotten. He is willing to deliver those people who are in captivity, those who are oppressed. And those in a wilderness . . . who are in faith . . . in sacrifice . . . in abandonment. Totally!

Here is the way out.

3

We now come to chapter three of Exodus. Moses is tending the sheep of his father-in-law. He does not know it but, in his desert experience, he is about to be called *to the Mountain of God*.

Moses is thinking only that he is keeping a flock which the Lord has entrusted to him. He does not know that he is being prepared to be the shepherd of *all* God's sheep!

Moses sees a flame of fire issuing from a burning bush and the burning bush is not consumed. Furthermore the Lord speaks to him out of this bush of flame. We know that this flame is the very love of God. This love is destined to be placed into the interior believer despite that believer's weaknesses.

It pleased your Lord to give a large portion of what He has burning within Him *to you*. This is what took place with Moses. Moses had a great flow of love. The first quality of the shepherd is love, for he must continuously risk his own life for that of the sheep.

The bush is now burning with a consuming fire and yet is not consumed. Here is a God who is filled with a Love that is never quenched. He is addressing a shepherd. He is demonstrating to that shepherd the love which the shepherd must have: an unequalled love; a love that is never tired and is never feeble.

You will discover that Moses was consumed with an inward, unquenchable fire of love for God's people. Later, when they were about to be smitten, it was *his* prayer which so touched the living God. Moses cried out, with pure, violent, love, "Lord forgive them. If it is necessary to blot someone out of the book of life, then let it be me." (Exodus 32)

Moses now sees this burning bush and dares to approach it. At that time the Lord tells Moses to take off his shoes for he is standing on holy ground. The Lord is saying to him, "Do not approach a love that is this pure, so extensive, and so unequalled, until you yourself are stripped of all other affection." Moses' feet represent other affections. Moses is to come naked to his God with nothing else in all the world that is his own. This alone is enough preparation for the task that is before him; in caring for this people in justice and equity, only love is needed. The ground of love is a holy thing. And it is from this central point that the shepherd will go out to judge with justice and holiness.

Now, at last, the Lord speaks to Moses about

delivering the people out of Egypt. Here we find the Lord telling Moses *the way out* of Egypt!

First the Lord says, "I am the God of Abraham, Isaac and Jacob. I have seen my people in Egypt. I have seen their suffering. I have heard their prayers. I know how severe their taskmasters are. And knowing their sorrows, I have now come down to deliver them out of Egypt, out of bondage, and out of their hyperactivity! I will, after many deliverances, take them into the good land."

Once more we are seeing God say to Moses, "You have sprung forth out of origins that were under My control. You are under My sovereignty. The Lord announces to Moses that Moses is going to go to Pharaoh and lead the people out. It will be Moses who will show them God's way out, and he will lead them into a region of peace and rest in God.

God allows Moses to know that He, the living God, has watched over these people, and known their afflictions. Moses now knows that their prayers have been heard by Him.

The Lord tells Moses to go to Pharaoh and deliver God's people. Moses, upon hearing this, protests that he simply cannot do such a great thing. The Lord responds, "I will be with you."

17

Moses protests, "I cannot do this which You have told me to do. I am incapable of it. The people are too great, the problems too great and the road too great. After all, can You expect a people of that size, such a multitude of people, to engage in blind abandonment to a God whom they cannot even see!" The thing that especially seems impossible to Moses is the thought of bringing these people out from under their present domination. It is difficult to draw souls from practices and methods which they have so long grown accustomed to . . . dare invite them to leave these habits, and this security, even though it be slavery, and walk out into a desert! An uncharted desert! The desert of faith!

But the Lord responds, "I will be with you, Moses! *I* will be the one who performs this great work!"

Moses continues his protestations. "What will happen when I go before the people of Israel and I say to them, 'The God of your fathers has sent me.' They will ask me, What is the name of this God? What shall I say to them then?"

Moses is saying, "If I go to those people and declare that I have come from the God of the people of Israel, or from the God of faith, or from the God of sacrifice, I am not sure what their response will be!" The Lord is not offended at Moses. Now observe what He tells Moses.

"*I AM THAT I AM* has sent you!" This is what Moses is to tell God's people. And what does this word mean? It means that He is a God of freedom. He is free of all things, . . . yet from Him none can be free. If you know yourself to be something and you have not seen that He is "I AM," then you are not fit to be one of His people. He is saying to them, "I am the truth; I am so much the truth that everything else is nothing. I look for a people who are nothing. I am the all."

The Lord is expecting them to see the need of laying aside their inventions, their conducts, and then to abandon themselves to this One who stretches from one eternity to the other; to give themselves utterly to one who encompasses all things; to come out of the land of man's industry; to follow in the way of abandonment.

If they will do this, surely they will find themselves conducted straight to Him. *He* will be *their way out*.

Now the Lord speaks again to Moses, "Tell my people that the God of Abraham, Isaac and Jacob has sent you to them."

Now here is reassurance! Your God was, and

is, Lord of Abraham! He is God of those who have *found* the way out! The God who leads you is the same God of the ancients. He walks in the same way, and has the same expectations.

Those who follow Him today as abandoned ones receive the same assurance which He gave Abraham and which He gave Moses. He will perform everything for you as He did for them.

His being is His name. His name is His being. Without Him, nothing exists. As His being apprehends and comprehends everything, so His name "I AM" expresses everything. Creatures are as nothing.

We need to have a name to distinguish ourselves from one another, but He who is truly *all* that is real has no need of such a distinction. The name I AM serves God. He needs no name. He is. He is all!

Those who see themselves as something rob Him of His name. Moses is assured, then, that those who follow the Lord are those who follow His name. At that name alone will His people obey His voice. You and I have the eternal God within us. Within you is the same voice of the one who is I AM.

The Lord now gives Moses very practical instructions. He is to gather up the elders of

Israel and go to the King of Egypt and tell Pharaoh that their God—the God of the Hebrews—has told them to go three days' journey out in the desert and make a sacrifice there to the living God.

A people telling the king that they are going out? And where are they going? To a desert! The desert of naked *faith*. And what will they do when they have gone into this desert? They will offer up a pure *sacrifice*.

The chapter closes with a very unusual and wonderful statement. "You will not leave Egypt empty-handed. You will despoil the very land that has held you captive."

The Lord is not content with giving you freedom, He will enrich you with the spoils, even the strengths, of those who would prevent you from entering into this pure way. As you leave, under the mighty hand of God, you will find that you have laid hold of strengths that are not yours. Your going out will become a strength you have never known! Those who see you go will lose strength proportionately.

"To him who has shall more be given, but for him who has not, what he has will be taken away."

4

Moses is having great difficulty bringing himself to enough faith to obey his God. He asks for a sign. To depend on a sign more than the speaking of God is a great fault — especially for one so advanced. Abraham, at one word from God, was willing to come up to the point of patricide.

See what God asks? "What is in your hand?" Moses had nothing in his hand. A rod only. Nothing! Leave Egypt only with what you have, be it no more than a stick. He will provide the remainder.

But even a miracle does not assure Moses. What is going on here? There is difficulty in becoming used to things that belong to other realms while one is still in this realm.

Until now the hesitation of Moses has been a more or less pure thing. Now he moves on to excuses: "I cannot speak." It is the property of the speaking of God to absorb our own.

The Lord reminds Moses who created his mouth, and who created it the *way* He has! He is introducing Moses to a higher understanding of sovereignty. Could a God who created his mouth ask him to speak if he could not? The leaving of Egypt and the wilderness are not too great for you if the Lord who created you says they are not!

The Lord makes known to Moses that the ability to speak of spiritual things resides not in the natural, but in the divine. The Lord will speak for Moses. And what does He ask of you? Whatever, it resides in the spiritual and not in *your* ability.

"I will be *in* your mouth." One who is sent (an apostolic person) has this advantage: God speaks by his mouth. Abandoned to Him in all things, He does not fail in this peculiar need.

Moses wants deliverance. But *his* very desire is a hindrance at this point. He is counseling God on how God can carry out the burden of Moses. All desire, even holy and just, ought to be banished from all annihilated souls. That soul ought to wish nothing but that which is the will of God. He brings to pass, in His time. The mark of annihilation is impotence to will or desire anything. The Lord was angry with him for coming out of total death to desire.

Until now Moses' words were spoken *in that* state of death. How dreadful it is to issue out of that state of abandonment. Moses gained a human mouth. Aaron.

Yet the Lord assures Moses, who is still maturing, that He will be with him.

The Lord now refers to Israel as "my first-born." This shows God's favor to those who prefer Him. Zipporah, the wife of Moses, even enters the scene. She calls "a bloody husband" as she beholds the circumcision taking place.

Zipporah does not understand the cross . . . nor does she wish to be made one with the cross, to share in His suffering. She leaves Moses at the first clear evidence of the cross in His life . . . not knowing that the cross is the beginning of rest.

The chapter ends with Israel receiving the word of present deliverance from their God. They believe! Moses has no difficulty in issuing God's word. Israel entered into His word.

Those who study the Scripture to know their God forget He is within their inmost being; intellectuals, those who travel the infinite corridors of reason, find Him not . . . for He is not *there*. And those who seek signs, *they* do not immediately give themselves up, but only yield by means of force. But those who believe, follow, and love . . . find.

5

Moses goes before Pharaoh and tells him what God has said, that Israel wishes to go and make a sacrifice to the Lord. Pharaoh gives us great insight into himself. He does not know the Lord, he says, which is very true, for only the simple in heart know Him, and do not know how to obey Him.

Pharaoh says it is because they have nothing else to do that the people wish to go and sacrifice to their Lord. They are too idle, he says. With nothing to do, therefore, they wish to make a sacrifice to their God.

Here is the typical attitude of those who accuse the interior believer of being idle. Sometimes this accusation comes from the world— from the *Pharaohs*—and sometimes it comes from spiritual directors, not understanding that this one has laid aside his life for prayer and for beholding the Lord, and that he has come to sacrifice his whole life to the Lord. The director who should know better says that this person is idle. Nonetheless, the Lord knows how to take care of His own, and to bring those who wish to live such a life into a secret place, where they cannot be disturbed by men.

Pharaoh's solution, of course, is to give them more work to do, to make them more external. Pharaoh is not the last to do this. Often the ministers of the Gospel load God's people down with all sorts of external things, never leading them to the internal.

This chapter tells us even more that when the Lord's people fail to do the external works, they are chastised, and even beaten. And though men may not be beaten with rods in our day, they are nonetheless told to feel guilty for not performing external services to the Lord. This is a Gospel, and an understanding of the Gospel, that is totally surface, and does not show us how much importance the Lord puts upon those who are friends of God by the way of the interior.

They are expected to perform as much as ever, and with even less. They have not even straw with which to build anymore. The more they strive to do things external, the less they are able to do. There is no rest, and there is no fruit. How typical of the one trying to live in the externals.

At this point in the record we find that the people are frustrated, and they remember that before Moses and Aaron came on the scene, though cruelty was great, it was not as great as it is now; that now they are being worked to death only because they had asked to go and sacrifice to their God.

Moses goes to the Lord with an inquiry: "Why, Lord, have You sent me to do this, when it has only brought affliction to your people?" Ever since he went before Pharaoh, the distress of the people has grown, and deliverance seems further away than ever before.

Although Moses is frustrated in this prayer, we see that he is a tenderhearted man, a tenderhearted and true shepherd, who is concerned about God's people. He is beseeching and exhorting the Lord to deliver the poor from tyranny.

When the moment comes in our lives that we seek to follow the Lord, when we seek to go out from Pharaoh, then and only then do we begin to push back the horizons of what God is really like. He is never what we imagined Him to be. The Lord had promised to deliver His people and to bring them out. Everyone thought, of course, that this meant that it would happen immediately. Moses does not know what lies ahead, nor do the people of God. Oh, how much poorer we would be today if all the hindrances that lay before Israel had been miraculously taken away. How much we learn from God when He waits. How much Israel learned about their

Lord in the days that followed. How much we all learn of what it means to come out.

We stand in greater awe when we realize that hundreds of thousands were delivered by the Lord's unusual providence, and yet of all those hundreds of thousands who were delivered from Egypt, yet only two entered the Promised Land. Who can understand the ways of God? (This we know, it is better to be in the wilderness, though one may go no farther, than to live in Egypt.) It is good and beautiful that His ways are hidden from the creature, even until they come forth in fact and reality. And His ways always come forth at the best possible moment — but it is always the moment that He alone chooses.

6

How encouraging it is to us to listen to God's reply to Moses. We see the weakness of the creature, and the greatness of the Creator. First of all the Lord simply tells Moses to be at peace, that He will behold what God will do. What simplicity!

Then the Lord simply declares who He is: the God of Abraham, Isaac, and Jacob, the God who has promised a land to His people. He is reminding Moses of faith, sacrifice, and abandonment. He reminds Moses that His name is Adonai. He calls on Moses to trust His sovereign hand and the ways that He Himself chooses. They will learn more of this—of the being of God—as they recognize more of their weakness and their nothingness.

The Lord is about to reveal Himself and greatly broaden Moses' view of what God is, and the people themselves will know so much more of their Lord. Not only that, but the Lord is providing a foundation for us, for He is giving to us Moses and the people of Israel as a perfect picture to show us what Jesus Christ is like. As God's people in Egypt accept more of their nothingness, they will enter into a perfect worship of the sovereignty of this holy Being.

These simple slaves and a wilderness shepherd named Moses will see more of the power of God than Abraham, Isaac and Jacob did, simply because "I have promised it."

The Lord's instructions to Moses are quite awesome. He tells Moses to go back and tell the people what he has already told them before, that "I the Lord will deliver the people out of the bonds of the Egyptians by a strong hand."

The Lord has heard their groanings; He has seen their willingness to abandon their lives to Him. He knows that He will stretch forth His hand and deliver them, and He will do it by extraordinary means.

Further, He assures them that they are going to know . . . not know by knowledge, but know by experience . . . that they belong to Him. The Lord always says to the abandoned souls that He will make them a peculiar people, and that He will be their God in a very particular way, and that they will know by experience that He is their God. Here is a promise reserved only for those who know abandonment and who without reserve give themselves to Him. He never allows Himself to be conquered by gifted ones. But He gives Himself up in a surpassing way to whosoever perfectly yields to Him.

Moses turns now and tells the people what the Lord has said. This time they are in such anguish of spirit and in so much exterior labor that they do not listen to the words of Moses. And so it is with the message of internal life. So many respond upon first hearing it; but afterward when suffering has come and the sweetness and the accompanying miracles are past, they find it very hard to follow the path when there is only a cross in view. This is an infidelity which is often committed by people who are first beginning to follow their Lord out.

Moses now turns to the Lord and tells the Lord that God's people are not listening. If Israel will not obey and respond, he says, then surely he has no hope when he goes before Pharaoh. If the righteous will not hear, certainly the wicked will not.

7

As Chapter 7 opens, the Lord is reassuring Moses by telling him, "When you stand before Pharaoh and he looks upon you, he will see you as one like unto a god, and he will see Aaron as a prophet of that god."

They may be cursed, they may be the off-scourge of the world; but those who walk the interior way are nonetheless looked upon with awe by the world. Somehow the world knows that these annihilated ones are speaking the very words of God and uttering, on behalf of others, the words pronounced by God Himself through empty vessels.

There is one other very interesting statement made in this chapter, found in verse 12. The magicians see the rod of Moses turned into a serpent. They are able to turn their rods into serpents also. Evil men can counterfeit things that are spiritual: the doctrine — and everything else, it would appear — at least at first glance. But just as Moses' rod, turned into a serpent, was able to eat up the counterfeit produced by the magicians, so those things that are of the Spirit of God absorb everything else and distinguish the false from the truth. The truth soon swallows up counterfeit spirituality.

8

As we read verse 17 of this chapter we see Aaron taking the dust of the earth and turning it to lice. The magicians cannot do this; therefore they declare, "Truly this is the finger of God!" And even though the magicians believe, yet Pharaoh's heart remains hardened. It is likewise true that all the marvels that God brings on behalf of the interior believer serve only to harden the hearts of his enemies. This seems impossible, but it is found to be true daily. Sometimes the most wicked are forced to confess that it is the finger of God, and yet you can be sure there are others standing in the very same place, witnessing and hearing the same miracles, whose hearts will be affected only by becoming more hardened than ever.

In verse 23, the Lord declares that He will put "a division between My people and your people."

How true! God separates His people from those who are not willing to be His. And while persecutors go through the agony of picking the lice of their vanity and their malice, and find that there is no rest in doing this unending task, the fortunate soul that belongs to God in a hidden way dwells content in a place of peace.

10

In Chapter 10 we find the amazing account of the heavens becoming darkened, and all of Egypt being filled with darkness. And yet it appears that there is light where the people of God dwell.

All who pretend to be in light, as the Egyptians did, but who walk in darkness find that the more they pretend to be in the light, the more ignorant they are.

When one is united to the Lord by faith alone, he dwells in light. Nothing can diminish this light. It is always a perfect day. Even when he seems to have lost all light, he is divinely enlightened. This is a matter that is not easily understood, and yet can be judged by those who are experienced in it. What you draw from God as your source is always true, for God is *truth* Himself. That which is drawn from the source of man, which is always based on our outward senses or our reasoning and our logic, is very often in error. Man, after all, is nothing but vanity and lies. The infallible way, then, for entering into truth is by dying and living. And that truth is to trust yourself only to God for all things, and to believe all things as they are seen from the eyes of God.

11

In Chapter 11:5 the Egyptians who die are the firstborn. An Egyptian firstborn is a figure of sin and sinners, for that which is sin can produce nothing but the sinner. The firstborn of God are always the interior souls, no matter what their birth order *or* gender.

The Egyptian wishes always to destroy the interior ones, because the Egyptian *is* external. But God, because He stands with those of the interior, humbles the sinner; and He slays the sin. It is the ministering angel of God who, using the power of God, puts to death the firstborn of the world.

Consider that, when you realize how esteemed are the *firstborn* of the *world*; they trust in things that are vain, whereas the firstborn of God are secure only in His protection. Egypt's firstborn are truly secure by the measure of men; but God's firstborn are mistreated by cruel men, though only so that they may receive a crown.

God's firstborn are never smitten because of His wrath, but only smitten in His mercy. It is the Egyptian who is smitten in wrath.

12

In this chapter we see that each family takes a lamb for his house, a lamb that is without blemish.

Interior believers can be distinguished only by the sign of God, and this sign is the blood of the Lamb. They are marked with this sign. And what do I mean by this? Having no other merit of their own, they possess everything in Christ Jesus. It is in His blood, and by His blood, that they are preserved. It is this blood which causes each of them to hope against hope. They despair of themselves, and this sends them happily to put perfect trust in God.

This lamb is without blemish, because in Jesus Christ there never was any sin, and it is His justice which obliterates our injustice.

After His people have eaten of the lamb, they take its blood and put it upon the doorpost. They roast this lamb with fire and eat it in the night before they go, along with unleavened bread and bitter herbs. *These* are the preparations for leaving Egypt. Here is part of *the way out*.

The way out demands that you must not only

be washed and marked with the blood of the Lamb; it is also necessary that you partake of His flesh. It is by partaking of Christ within you that you grow and become fruitful. Here is strength for you to pass out of Egypt and out into the fearsome desert of naked faith.

And although you will find freedom out in that desert, and many heavenly sweetnesses that will sustain you on a hard pilgrimage, nonetheless that desert is a far more difficult place to bear than your first captivity.

You see, a love of *self* actually *prefers* to be *burdened* with labor, activity and *even* with making bricks, rather than to be free and employed in possessing heavenly realms (the Promised Land, and the Lord Himself). To be taken with the things of conquering the heavenly realm strikes at the very nature of the self life because—if for no other reason—there are no outward results from this type of work. A love of self likes to see what it has accomplished, in measurable external ways.

The bitter herbs remind us of things past which were bitter, and also remind us of the things that must be put to death within us as we move out into faith. When you enter into the desert of faith, you will pass through many mortifications.

This is all Part of dieing to self. Very difficult!

44

The *unleavened bread* is made with very little preparation. It is oil and flour that has been cooked; nothing else is added. This is the simple life, the *simple* state of the believer. He will have simple nourishment from now on. There are no elaborate preparations for this nourishment. There is nothing in it that is corrupting, and neither is there anything in it that is delightful and sweet. Ahead is simple sustenance, the simple sustenance of the Lord Jesus — not elaborate as most men partake of Him in their religious rituals.

As to the flesh of the lamb, note that it is made with fire and it is roasted. It is not boiled, nor fried, but *roasted* — the highest kind of preparation of this food. When you consume Christ in this way, the fire of the Lord comes into you. There is a fire of love; we are set on fire by partaking of, and eating, this Lamb, who is without blemish.

Now the Lord's people are told that they are to eat everything of the lamb, and if anything is left over when morning arrives it is to be burned with fire. It is so obvious that we are seeing here in this Jewish feast a picture of the coming of the Lord Jesus Christ as He gives Himself as food to us.

But there is something else here, and that is

a reminder that our sacrifice, too, must be pure, as His was. The soul must be consummated into God out there . . . in the *desert* of faith.

The sacrifice must be *entire*; there can be no reservation, nothing held back. It is a burnt offering that is wholly burned; nothing is left. Everything must be consumed and devoured: the head, the feet, the inward parts, the most interior depths of the soul — all must be destroyed so that there may be nothing remaining whatsoever, either inwardly or outwardly.

The Lord's people are told that even the most inward parts, even the entrails, must be burned. Here is a complete sacrifice. But do not be deceived. How difficult is this sacrifice! How much more it costs the soul than can ever be described! How much sacrifice there is before surrender itself comes!

And where are those, where is that one who reserves nothing?

As difficult as it is, and as rare as it is, yet all the half-sacrifices can never measure up to this holocaust. Here is a sacrifice which God peculiarly reserves to Himself — a consecration which He made to His glory alone, and He calls others to this pure sacrifice, which is uniquely His.

It is a deplorable thing that many well-known

and illustrious Christians have allowed themselves to be sacrificed in so many ways, yet reserve their "entrails" — *their inmost parts* — as *unsacrificed*. Oh, if they knew the glory which God draws from the *pure* and *total* sacrifice, and the advantage which would come to them from making such a sacrifice! How much more generous they would become by abandoning themselves without reserve.

In this world, so often it is said, "Oh, look at the great loss," when what they are actually beholding is *gain*. And so often it is said, "Oh, what gain," when actually they are beholding so great a *loss*. To lose all for God is to gain everything. To lose everything with regard to ourselves, to let Him take us into His sovereign glory without mixture or any personal interest at all — that is the supreme way and the most sublime witness of pure love.

But *pure sacrifice* is God's sacrifice reserved for Him alone. It is the divine sacrifice of Jesus Christ. All others are modeled after it. In this sacrifice He wills that all things be destroyed.

Oh, spotless victim! It is Your total immolation, oh Lord, which all pure sacrifices are composed of. *You* are the origin of them, and the spirit and the power and the perfection of all sacrifices are found in Your sacrifice. All other sacrifices are but *pictures* of the pure and total sacrifice. In all others there is something which the creature desires and expects to receive. There is something that the creature wishes to be reckoned to him.

Now we see the Lord telling the people to leave eating. We get out by simply partaking of Jesus Christ!

He then gives them even more instructions on "the way out." He says to them: "Gird up your loins, have your shoes on your feet, have your staff in your hand, eat as you go." This is the Passover, this is the passage of God.

What does it mean to gird up your loins? This denotes the purity of obedience to God's will. It is a happy binding. An *outward* purity of the *flesh* is but the figure of *interior* purity, which is of the *spirit*. Men today are so quick to be *outwardly* pure in the things they do and do not do, not realizing that this is but a *symbol*, an inference, of what should be *within*. There must be a purity of the spirit. *All outward purity* emanates from an *inward purity*. And if we wash only the outside, the *inward* remains *corrupt*. All things must begin from *within* and work outward.

Interior purity consists in conformity to the

will of God. The more imminent this conformity, the purer the spirit.

This can be clearly traced. First of all, the will
of the believer is rendered conformed to the will
of the Lord in all things. Secondly, the will of
the believer becomes uniform with that of the
Lord. And afterwards it is transformed into the
will of God. It is at this point that all will of
the self is dead, and must be destroyed, and pass
as ashes into the divine will. From this point we
are no longer speaking of anything but the very
will of God Himself: His will . . . in Him and
in the creature.

And what shall we say of the feet? We saw
that Moses had to take off his shoes before the
burning bush. But here we see the shoes are on
the feet, and this represents a pilgrimage. The
Old Testament believer is eating the lamb in
haste. A passage is about to be made. The pure
sacrifice is being consumed within them, and it
is doing its annihilating will. And the feet are
shod; this means that the soul is passing into
God. There is a nothingness here, and the Lord
is becoming the fullness of this immense void.

In the true consuming of a sacrifice, a void
can only be filled by God Himself; if anything
else fills it, it is not a true and pure sacrifice.
The Lord empties the soul of sin; in proportion

as He does, He fills that soul with gifts and graces. Then He empties that same soul of His gifts and graces, in order to fill it with Himself alone. And this emptying serves to take away from the soul its natural ability to be enlarged. The natural man is softened and opened to the penetration of divine Life.

Now after this must come a removal of the residue of the infection of sin. For this He prepares a fire. This fire is subtle, but it is also more devouring. The fire seems to damage the soul instead of purifying it. The beauty of this work can only be seen after it is accomplished, not during that time. It is necessary that the fire take away the radical residue of the soul, so that there be no impurities left. If you cannot see the impurities in your own life now, and how deep and howsubtle they are, it is more clear than ever that such an operation must take place in your life.

When this faithful soul has arrived at a total loss of its propriety and restriction, then that soul is becoming ready for union . . . that is, for intimate unity.

As I have said, He leaves nothing void, and He fills the void of that believer's faculties with His gifts; then He takes the gifts away and fills the void with Himself.

A total void can only be filled by the uncreated

All. He enlarges the capacity of the soul to receive, in proportion to the filling, and He fills in proportion to the enlargement. There is no emptiness ever in the soul.

Can the soul contract and be enlarged? This is the question. When there is hardness in the soul, it seems to be torn to pieces when it is enlarged to receive more of the Lord. But the believer must realize that is exactly what is taking place — enlargement, for more of Christ. The more the believer allows the soul to be torn, the more quickly the operation is done.

It is my observation that it is very difficult for the believer to submit to these enlargements and contractions. He seeks to be sheltered from the seeming damage of this as much as possible. And although the believer is convinced of the truth that has been stated here, he sadly fails in practicing . . . fails far beyond all that can be imagined! The more the soul resists, the more it prolongs the pain. Many, therefore, because of unfaithfulness, never arrive at this life of utter void and utter possession.

There are those whose lives are passed in building and destroying, not being able to suffer a void within themselves. The moment the void comes there is immediate filling up with their own industry — a desire in truth to acquire everything and lose nothing. The depths of the divine Life and the walk of that life are never given to a soul in completeness until there is a void place for that Life to move into.

Almost no one gives himself up to this, and those who have experienced what I am speaking of understand what I am saying perfectly.

Now in verse 15 the Lord tells the people to eat unleavened bread for seven days, and during that time, there is to be no leavened bread in their homes.

I see this as a significant period of time. Perhaps we are seeing here a reference to a period of seven years, in which the soul of the believer must pass through a losing period — the losing of its own inventions little by little — before it is possible to enter into the desert of naked faith. The Lord makes it very clear that those who preserve the leavened bread and eat the leavened bread will be cut off from Israel — that is, they will never be able to obtain a purified interior.

In verse 23 the Lord makes a promise that He will smite the Egyptians, and when He sees the blood on the doorpost, He will pass over that door and will not destroy those within. There is nothing to fear for those who are marked with the seal and with the blood of the Lord Jesus Christ. He is faithful to those who are on their way out of Egypt, who have put their confidence only in His blood, and in nothing else; who by the loss of all self-righteousness find themselves happily obliged to despair entirely of that which is within themselves. They are more safe than if they possessed all things, because they are marked with His blood; and this blood is the totality of all their merit. There is no other merit.

Then the Lord says to them, "In the years to come your children will ask, 'What was this Passover? What kind of worship was this? What did you do there?' And you will reply, 'This was the Passover, when the Lord passed over us and smote the Egyptians.'"

What manner of glorifying God is this?

Say to them when they ask "What is this?" that here is the pure sacrifice of the Lord, which is reserved for Himself alone. It is the mark of passage on the way out, when the soul has passed into Him with the loss of all propriety. And in that hour the truly interior person will do as the Hebrews did; he will bow his head and will submit and will worship at this fact: that it is the taking of all from the creature to restore the all to God.

The Lord tells Moses that this is the way that the Passover is to be conducted and that no stranger shall eat of it. I see this as the state of the soul in a mysterious passage — passing from Egypt out into the desert of naked faith. If a believer is not fully the Lord's this experience will remain something he cannot understand and cannot partake of. Only abandonment allows the proper eating. Here is a nourishment that is simple, bitter and difficult — a state that is denuded. It cannot be relished by strangers, nor can it sustain them. Thus do not be surprised if such ones cannot even comprehend it. But for those called and those chosen, here truly is a delicious food.

Now we come to a very interesting and crucial point. Strangers are not to eat of this food nor make this passage unless they are circumcised. There are those who have been brought to see the interior way by people who are particularly chosen of the Lord to share such matters. Such ones eat of this way. But there is also a hireling. He seeks his own interests. He cannot eat of this, for he asked to eat of it *only* because he negotiates in hopes for personal gain. He is forbidden.

And if a stranger does come and desires to join with them and to enter into this state, let him first cut off all that he still has of his old practices. Let him come and associate with them only after retrenchment from Egypt. Let him enter into the same state with them and there partake of the *passage food*.

Now in verse 49 the Lord tells us that there is only one law, both for the sojourner and for those born in the land (those who come easily into the ways of His Kingdom, and those who find it difficult). For both there is a mysterious annihilation of things interior, an indispensable passage for both. The Lord will not change the law of things that are spiritual.

13

There is an interesting thing the Lord does in the seventeenth verse. He declares that He will not allow His people, just come out of Egypt, to escape to the land of the Philistines; then He gives His reason: If God's people go through a battle at this time, they will become so discouraged that they will return to Egypt.

Those who begin their journey out of the land of Egypt and who have just walked into the desert of faith rarely go through any great duress at this time. There are many things already on them to endure. To encounter the Philistines, to encounter the powers of darkness now would be a great loss. *If* temptation begins to attack them in the very *beginning*, there is an excellent chance they will return to their old practices. A little time is needed for them to be confirmed in this new way in which they are walking.

Rather than going to the land of the Philistines, they must take a longer route. As the people walk out into the desert, they do not meet war, for, from this moment on, it is the Lord who will fight for them. Others may fight battles and grace may sustain them, but in this new life of faith it is not so. The soul is quite weak, very susceptible to love, but not strong for battle. It is better to go through the desert of faith than it is to go through some trial of war. It may seem to you that the desert is safer. Actually, the route through the desert is both longer and more painful.

Now watch them walk out into the desert, where there are no landmarks. They look into the sky and they see a cloud. There will be light by day and there will be light by night. This is the Lord Himself, who is caring for these abandoned ones. They have nothing now but Him. He will care for them and He will lead them. He does not leave them even for a moment. Upon stepping out into the sands, they look up and realize that *He* is leading them. For the first time, they are learning to follow a Lord of light and guidance.

And what does this mean for you today as you walk out into the desert of faith? It means there is a light within you, there is a cloud and a pillar of fire. The internal, indwelling Christ is there to lead you. You will not look any longer at objective things to lead you. Outward and external things will find less and less place in the Lord's leadership. You will follow a cloud and a pillar of fire.

This is not a distinct light; it is quite indistinct.

This is to keep the soul from being easily distracted: distracted *by knowing too much* of what it is the Lord is doing.

The God who tempers the heat of the day also dissipates a little of the darkness of the night that is found in the desert. This grace given by God is one of the things which allows the soul to be preserved in this frightful desert. The cloud and the fire do not fail him who dares step out of Egypt and follow the way out through the desert of faith in Him.

14

Now the Lord's people have left Egypt, and the first trial of the desert of faith is upon them. They must move from fear to fact. The Egyptians are chasing them, and they are very much afraid. They say to Moses, "Were there not enough graves in Egypt? Why did you bring us into this place to die?"

The way of faith is new to them. They are novices. They do not know the ways of the Lord. There are very few sufficiently abandoned to Him not to regret their decision and their first encounter with the desert. On the one hand they are about to fall into the hands of the enemy, on the other they are about to be drowned in the sea. Death appears certain. So if death is certain, why not then have died in Egypt? Egypt is far better!

Moses says to them, "Do not be afraid."

And I would say, dear friend, "Be not afraid." Death is inevitable; you cannot be delivered from it. Your strength has been taken from you, nor will you find help in any other living creature. Your Lord knows a way out, right through the frightful sea. You have but one care, and that is *not* to leave the state of abandon.

At this point the soul cannot remember the miracles. All is dark. The anguish is beyond all that can be expressed, and everything is painted with the image and shadow of death.

Courage, dear soul. You have come to the edge of the Red Sea, where soon you will see the enemy receive his reward. Follow on your present path. Remain immovable, like a rock. Do not find a pretext to stir from where you are.

The Lord will fight for you now. Many people break down at this place. They do not find the way out. They stop here and never advance.

It is important, if you are one helping another Christian at this point, to have love and patience, to bear all complaints which issue from their fear of loss.

Moses does not know what to do, and he turns to the Lord. The Lord says, "Why talk to Me? Tell My people to go forward." His goodness and His power shine forth in the moment of extreme need. What do you need at this point? Courage and abandon are all that are necessary. And this profound sea, which engulfs all others, will be found dried up for the true abandoned ones. They will find life where others find death. You need only go forward.

Moses had to make a decision. The decision entailed the possibility of walking over on dry land. It is necessary that your spirit be separated from your external senses. When that division is made, the soul can walk in a blind abandon and happily press the sea. That which is a rock of destruction to others is the port of safety to such a one.

And now the angel of the Lord appears, and the Egyptians are on one side of the angel and God's people are on the other, so that the two armies cannot come near one another during the night.

Here is a beautiful picture of support that comes only from God. Israel has no other. Even here they are aware of little or no divine support. This is the proper disposition with which to enter the sea — without assurance of support, and facing loss. They now seem to have nothing of God. There is nothing of Him that is known to them. Yet behind them is the angel of God, unseen, protecting them. *They have never been so protected as now.* Such is His way with those on their way out. The Lord takes away the powers of Satan over such souls.

Now Moses lifts up the rod and a great wind begins to blow. The sea dries up and the water divides. His people walk over on dry land.

Please notice that it is the Holy Spirit that makes the separation between the two parts — that which is the animal part of us and that which is the spiritual part of us. Water here serves as a wall to protect God's chosen people. Water which naturally is a thing of death shelters and guarantees safety from an attack. But note one thing: that it was Moses who stretched forth his hand to give the signal for the division of the two parts. The Holy Spirit did the work.

The division of self is not done by human means; this is reserved for the Holy Spirit alone. In the desert of faith, the burning winds in the midst of an obscure night dry up the dangerous waters. He divides the deep and rich spirit from the outward, exterior senses. He divides soul from spirit. This can be done so easily when the soul is reduced to its last state of exhaustion. When the soul is in the state of extreme dryness by loss of its interior abilities and all the powers of its facilities. It is in times when such universal dryness causes everything to flow to the center that the Spirit can sometimes be best discerned.

Now the Egyptians come hard after the people of God with chariots and horses. Then comes the intervention of the Lord. All Egypt is enveloped in the midst of great waves.

When the Egyptian soul comes to face this

hour, he may believe that he, too, can go over on dry land. But he will be taken in and engulfed by the waves.

It is the Lord alone who can issue the divine call to go forth. It is the Lord alone who draws up the soul and reduces it to nothing. It is He, when He is the authority and He is the spiritual director, who causes these things to come to pass. The only element lacking in the way out, at this point, is for the soul to give full consent to everything that it may please God to let befall that soul, whether it is something the soul knows or does not know.

15

Salvation has come and suddenly the people of God break out in a triumph praise. As they see the horses and the riders have been thrown into the sea by the Lord, then a psalm of thanksgiving rises.

The soul, whose eyes are open, sings to the Lord a new song after such a great initial deliverance. Here is the first true happiness of deliverance. Such an experience must come to all faithful and abandoned ones. Until now there have been miracles and extraordinary providence, but the eyes of God's people were not sufficiently opened to the marvels of God. Now they are, and they sing and praise and give thanks with inspiration. They have come to understand some of the attributes of God, and they attribute all that has happened to them to this God. Faithfully they render to Him all the glory for what He has done on their behalf.

Abandoned ones are praising ones.

Now in verse 22 we see that having passed through the sea, they go into the desert of Shur. They walk for three days in the desert and they find no water. This people who are following

Moses and following God will eventually have a very strong foundation to pass through the blistering desert that lies before them. But that firm establishment has not yet arrived. Things which are far more appalling than three days without water lie ahead of them.

We always think, when we have come out of Egypt and passed through a sea of death, that this is the end of our miseries! Yes, it seems we *always* think this. In fact, calamities are but the beginning! We have enjoyed a new life, we have enjoyed comfort—everything seems to be accomplished. Our problems are now behind us. But to have *found* God is not to have completely possessed God. And further, this state is certainly not a state where we ourselves are possessed by Him. Such a state demands a love that has enormous purity in it—far more than these people, three days out of Egypt, possess.

It is astounding that so many people have the courage to pass through the Red Sea, yet so few people are found who can venture to pass what follows *after* the Red Sea! We shall see this clearly.

It is necessary for you to be free from all *external* activities and all external *interests*, and to never begin again anything of that which you have left behind.

You must know that in all the many states that are involved in the *interior life*, each new stage, each new level, is *preceded* by a sacrifice. Then comes an *abandon*, and following that is always a state of utter *destitution*. Nor does this occur in your life only once, but over and over again, as you are brought further and further into the Lord.

In the course of the purifying of your love toward the Lord, your soul enters first by *sacrifice* — that is, the lifting up of itself to God. *Afterwards* the soul *abandons itself* to Him. Then it leaves itself *destitute* before Him — or is *left* destitute before Him — or, perhaps, by Him.

The depths of each stage come according to the capacity and the light that is given the believer in each stage.

Eventually the soul of the believer enters the state that I call "naked faith." Here the believer finds his soul so different from others and from his past state that he makes yet a new sacrifice: to remain in a constant state of sacrifice, abandonment and destitution.

You might think that at this point such a believer would have advanced to a state of interior maturity; however, the very *opposite* is true. He returns from manhood to infancy — almost to the state of being born anew.

Now, some do leave themselves destitute, but only in *one area* and *not* in another! And some who do so very well in one area fail in another. The greater part of those who give themselves to the interior walk withdraw after having given themselves up to it. Or they retain something of themselves in some area.

Having said that, it is with assurance that I say that after the Red Sea there is *always* a desert. It is a strange place, with a strange appearance, which has to be passed through. The length of the coming destitution will be so tedious that the greater number will tire of it.

In the meantime the soul of the believer has no longer any possession here for itself. Therefore nothing satisfies the soul, and it finds itself in a desert without water. The believer is quite sure that he will die of thirst.

The people of God now come to Marah. The water there is bitter, and they wonder what they will drink.

Whatever water *is* given from high realms at this point is so bitter it cannot be drunk, and therefore murmuring arises. It is certain that many do not sin in this outburst of murmuring. Theirs is the instinct of survival; this is not a murmuring within the spirit. Nonetheless, it is also true that the natural instincts of survival may attack the spirit, and this murmuring can move from an instinctive matter of survival and *become* a bitterness and rebellion. This may be difficult to understand, but *murmuring* can take place *in a state of abandon*! (It does not take place in a state of destitution.)

Now the Lord shows Moses a tree; the tree is cast into the water and makes the water sweet.

We are seeing here the tree of the cross which is cast into the water of bitterness and which has the power to sweeten that which is bitter. Those things that come into our lives have been rendered less severe by the cross. The Lord gives relief to the soul in this horrible desert, and there comes relief through the sweetness of the cross.

This is difficult to understand for those who have not experienced it.

Shall it be understood that in a state of nothingness, in the desert of faith, where the soul experiences neither pain nor pleasure, that in order to relieve the soul of this difficulty, suffering is brought in! What a paradox! Yet self-love is strange. It is so envious of possessing something . . . anything . . . that it prefers rather to *suffer* than to have *nothing*! It would rather suffer a grievous ill than to feel neither good nor evil. It must sense *something*!

Those who have experienced this state, this

beginning taste of nothingness, will confess that what I say here is the truth. There is nothing so frightful as *nothingness*. And if we subsist on something, no matter how horrible its pain, we are more content than with having the sense of nothing.

We see then a most unusual thing: that God is bestowing, here on the soul of the believer, *comfort*. It is a comfort that is suffering! Suffering which waters the soul of the believer and, therefore gives consolation.

Soon the Lord's people come to Elim where there are twelve springs of water and seventy palm trees. After the Red Sea, after much labor and affliction, the Lord will give a time of healing. There is always a place of refreshment, where there is shade and water. It is the Lord's way to give some relief after the trial of the cross.

The soul that is not greatly experienced in the Lord's ways imagines that it has already obtained the victory at this point. Yes, it is true that the things of the world and the things of the realms of darkness may be in the Red Sea. But there is still the Lord to contend with. He does much trying of the believer.

Note that there are twelve wells here, one for each tribe. Twelve wells for twelve tribes make up, nonetheless, only one band of interior people. These twelve springs are the Lord Jesus Christ flowing out of the deep parts of Himself into the deep parts which are *inside* the faithful ones.

16

After leaving Elim, the Hebrews, hungry and without food, grumbled against the Lord and against Moses. They would rather have died in Egypt, they said, where they had plenty to eat, than die of hunger in the wilderness. The Lord sent manna for their food.

A man trying to live by his own strength, apart from the spirit, is actually weak and foolish. Nevertheless, a mature Christian has the responsibility for such weak ones, and I urge you to be patient with them. They are beginning to discover how *little* they have to offer the Lord (or anyone else for that matter) and are finding that fact hard to bear. Their natural unfaithfulness hinders them from remaining in the passive state God desires for them. They blame their teachers and advisers for their discomfort. They miss the light and sweetness they used to experience in the Lord. What they do not realize is that the *fervor* they felt for the Lord in that delightful state was more *sensual* than *spiritual*.

It is so difficult for us fleshly beings to become spiritual, and to content ourselves with faith in God alone! We often leave our internal walk for periods of time—not because we want to, but simply because our fleshly nature, suffering at being deprived, gains the upper hand and does what it wishes.

Many who are progressing in the inner way are unaware of what is happening. They think that they were more pleasing to the Lord in their earlier, more enjoyable state. They think, "If only I had died *then*, my state before God would have been far better than now."

We see the goodness of God, who repaid the grumbling of this people — with *heavenly manna*. This very recompense, this nourishment, which God bestowed on them, shows that their discontent was not an act of their will.

You who may be older and more mature in the Lord, who have persons like this under your care — have compassion on them. They are worthy of it. Treat them as God treats them; and above all, encourage them to continue seeking the Lord within. The weaker they appear, the more they need fellowship with their Lord to nourish and strengthen them. Like manna, the Lord desires them to receive *Him* as nourishment *every day*, as long as they are needy, in order, as He says, "that I may test them, whether or not they will walk in My instruction."

This is the only test God desires of these faithful souls at this time. Their test is whether or not they will receive the *blessings* that God is offering them. They are often tempted, because of their sufferings, to withdraw from their close walk with the Lord; but God desires to test them, to see if they will faithfully receive Him every day. This is His way of proving their obedience. He wants to see if they will obey in spite of their own reluctance, and at the same time are willing to admit their reluctance.

The Lord gives *days of rest* when we are deterred by *God Himself* from gathering the manna He has already provided for us. But this state is only temporary. The Lord gives a brief rest, then He returns the believer to daily labor for his food. Nevertheless the believer continues to live on the hidden manna he received, and to draw from it a double grace. Such times of rest in God bring the believer more than his own labors can.

The patience of God toward such weak believers should serve as an example to all who have young saints in their care. It is a sure mark of a person's advancement not to be astonished or annoyed at seeing others' weaknesses, and to judge them according to truth. Instead, those who are unenlightened load the weak ones with reproaches and penances. Such unsympathetic teachers discourage them from going on, by making perfection seem an impossible goal.

In the manna from heaven, what a picture we see of the inner partaking of Christ! What a glorious mystery, that the one who receives only a small portion has *no less* of the reality of Christ within than he who receives more. And the one who takes a greater part has no more than he who partook of less. Each one receives no more, no less than what he can eat — in other words, *all* of Jesus Christ, *all* contained in the smallest as well as the greatest portion.

In this wonderful reality of the manna, oh Lord, You give Yourself wholly to everyone who seeks You.

This is also a picture of the Divine state; *every* believer has the *fulness of Christ's life* — each according to his capacity. The beginner is full, as well as the more advanced. Although the more mature Christian has a greater capacity and can hold more of God, nevertheless it is the same God who is all in all, and all in each of them. He alone can form their fulness and true satisfaction.

17

The Israelites grumbled, accusing Moses of bringing them out of Egypt to die of thirst in the wilderness. The Lord promised to give Moses a special rock; Moses struck the rock, and water poured forth from it.

The distressful thirst which must be endured on this road is a picture of self-love. This people, chosen and cherished, murmured against God. But God, out of His infinite goodness, did not grow tired of providing for them. The rock gave forth water (the waters of grace) to relieve them; and God stood over this rock, for He is the source of this grace. It is very difficult to remain fully yielded to the Lord, and there will always be those who — now and then — withdraw themselves. Yet God causes water to issue out of the rock, as a proof of the unchangeableness of His blessings towards those very persons who are sometimes unfaithful to Him.

Moses gave a true name to this people's *fault* when he called it *temptation*, for they said, "We shall see if the Lord is with us or not." They were testing their Lord.

It is impossible not to desire signs, particularly when we are led, as these people were, through the wilderness. *Doubt* causes us to *vacillate*. We are not able to allow ourselves to be entirely stripped. This makes our time in the desert *all the longer*. For this reason almost all die on the road before arriving at the Promised Land.

The Israelites faced a formidable enemy, the Amalekites, and Moses sent Joshua to fight against them, while Moses stood on a hill. Whenever he held out his hands, Israel prevailed, but when he dropped his hands, Amalek prevailed. Aaron and Hur stationed themselves on either side of Moses to support his hands, and thus Joshua defeated Amalek.

For those called to follow the Lord, there are bound to be persecutions. The natural man makes war on this people, wishing to destroy them. The lifting of Moses' hands represents our *faithfulness* in remaining *elevated to God* by abandon and faith, and our determination to look *only* upon God, whatever enemies we may have. And while in this state we easily gain the victory.

But when Moses lowers his hands — that is, when we relapse into self-absorption — we are immediately vanquished. Our self nature, finding itself plunged into its weakness, is lost in vain turnings and windings from the moment it begins to regard itself rather than God. From that time we enter into doubt and hesitation, into pain and trouble — which bring about our defeat. In this state Amalek (who denotes natural and self love, which are the only enemies that remain to the believer who has come this far) immediately gains the advantage.

To avoid such defeat, we must simply remain seated upon the rock — hold ourselves firmly in a yielded state and dwell in the repose of abandon — while faith and confidence, as hands held up towards God, sustain us in our distress.

18

Moses' father-in-law Jethro came to the camp of the Israelites in the desert, and saw Moses bearing the whole load in secular matters as well as spiritual. He advised Moses to appoint able men to handle lesser problems and disputes, so that Moses could save his strength for spiritual leadership. Moses accepted Jethro's advice and put it into practice.

Jethro's counsel was an excellent one for spiritual advisers, and there are two important rules to be learned here.

First, Jethro instructed Moses that his duty (and that of spiritual leaders in general) was to stay out of the mundane affairs of his people, and to devote himself to the glory of God in them and to their perfection, leaving day to day matters to others. Thus the spiritual leaders would not be overtaxed with this burden, which would rob them of the time they need to give to things of eternal consequence. Furthermore, since God has not required them to handle temporal matters, they should not interfere in them.

Secondly, there is a wonderful example here in Moses' humble acceptance of his father-in-law's counsel. Although Moses was so full of the spirit of God, and Jethro was not even of his people, it is necessary to receive truth and good counsel wherever they come from. God often sends vessels much inferior in dignity and grace to show leaders that it is He alone who is the author of all good light.

19

The Israelites made camp in front of Mt. Sinai. Moses went up the mountain where God spoke to him, saying that if the Israelites would obey His voice and keep His covenant, they would be His people, they would be a kingdom of priests and a holy nation. Moses reported these words to the elders of the people. Then the Lord came to Moses in a thick cloud and instructed the people not to approach the mountain or they would die.

God, in His tender care, provides a teacher (or counselor) to those whom He conducts in faith; He does this to help them understand the will of the Lord. Although all peoples belong to God, the interior people are His people in a special way. This means that if they will yield themselves completely to God, they will become so fully God's that nothing else can find any place in them. God says that they will be chosen from among all peoples.

In order for God's people, who are so dear to Him, to arrive at such a blessed state, all He asks of them is that they obey Him and remain yielded to Him. The expression, "keep My covenant," could be expressed, "remain in My union."

The "kingdom" denotes the absolute power that God possesses over souls who offer him no resistance in anything. He is utterly their master. It is not the same with others — with those who possess themselves — because, being full of self-will, they desire a thousand good things which God does not desire for them. He grants them these things only because of their *weakness*; but He reigns as king over those who have *no more will of their own.*

Therefore, when He taught His disciples to pray and to ask that His kingdom might come (that is, that He might reign absolutely over them) He also added that His will might be done on earth *as in heaven.* This was a prayer that the Lord's will might be done on the earth as the blessed do it in the heavenlies, without resistance, without hesitation, without exception, and without delay.

The Lord added to Moses that His people would be a "priestly kingdom," for this kingdom is formed of priests. They would be unto Him a truly holy nation; after all the wickedness of man had been destroyed in them, nothing would remain in them but the holiness of God. They would be holy for God, and not for themselves.

God did not say simply, "You shall be a holy nation," but "You shall be *unto Me* a holy nation."

When God's people first heard of the way He wanted to lead them, they gave their consent *unanimously*, offering themselves as a gift and a sacrifice. God is so good that He seeks *our consent* before He introduces us into His ways, which, He warns us, will involve loneliness and suffering. Although He is sovereign ruler, He governs with a great reserve, respecting our free will. But once we feel a little pain, we tend to forget our consent and our sacrifice!

How willingly and promptly we offer to sacrifice ourselves! In our fervor we forget our weakness, our distaste for suffering. We immediately reply, like this people, "We will do whatever You wish." If only we stopped at that moment to consider our powerlessness, we would realize that we can do *nothing* of ourselves. And if we remembered our abandon to God, we would know that we have no will left — *not even the will to leave ourselves entirely in God's hands!* At this point, the best thing we could say would be, "Let the Lord cause us to do everything, and we will do it, for our trust is in Him. Of ourselves we are weak and sinful." But to be confident in, to lean on, one's self (which is a secret pride) is always followed by a fall.

The "darkness of a cloud" shows that God desires His interior people to believe (on the basis of faith alone) that it is He who speaks to direct us; we should not depend upon *signs*!

This sanctification which God desires is a new purity, in order to enter into a new state, governed by a new law — that of pure love.

Moses, having already passed through the state of death, was allowed to stand on the mountain where God was — God who is the origin of this state of pure love. He, because he was already purified, was conducted to love's very source.

If anyone else tried to touch this mountain, or even to approach it, it would cost him his life. The Lord Himself says: "No man shall see me and live."

But how would he die? It would not be by the hand of man; God Himself would send arrows to pierce his heart, because no one can love the Lord purely without losing his own life. God will crush him with stones, because his heart, which has not allowed itself to be softened by the blessings God pours out on it, is but a heart of stone. God must take from him this heart of stone in order to give him a heart of flesh, capable of pure love — a heart pliable and easily handled, a heart pure and new.

Many would like to think that the Word of God is all sweetness. Indeed, that is true if His Word is considered in itself, or when it is accompanied by a tender outpouring of grace, such as is found in the *beginnings* of the spiritual life! *Then* it is sweet and agreeable. But later for souls being dealt with by the Lord, the Word of God can be terrifying . . . seeming to hold only bitterness.

When God first appeared to Moses, in the burning bush, Moses was not allowed to approach the fire without taking off his shoes. At Sinai He invites Moses *into* the *fire itself.* This is possible because of the purity of Moses' love, which has infinitely increased. When God formerly appeared to this faithful minister to impart to him His true love, it was in the fire. Now that He desires to give the law of pure love, He appears also to the children of Israel in the very fire of love, since He is love itself. It requires no less a fire to kindle so many hearts.

But how can it be, my Love, that You appear here so terrible? You appear so to those who see You only outwardly and in the effects of Your love, which, superficially, appears cruel towards the souls that are devoted to You; but inwardly and in itself, there is no doubt that Your love is agreeable to the yielded heart.

How wonderful, that God speaks to the believer and the believer hears Him! The believer speaks to God and God also hears him! But there is much else that goes on between God and the individual believer which no one else knows about. To accomplish this, God causes this chosen one to mount up to the summit of the mountain of love. He is received into God Himself, but in a manner so sublime and so ineffable that there is no way to describe it.

At such a time, all that remains in the exterior (or lower part of man) is changed and renewed by the purity of such love. This man is saturated with the divine, not only within, but even outwardly. These saints, or rather this one saint from among so many millions of saints, not only ascend the mountain, but go up to the very top of the mountain; for it was necessary that he should be provided with this pure love, both for himself and others. He must draw it up from this source of fire, becoming a furnace capable of spreading the holy fire to many people.

We see Moses in a changed condition. Once, in his humility, he counted himself unworthy to speak to Pharaoh and to the people of Israel. Now, in his profound annihilation, he ascends without pain or reluctance to the highest degree in God, to speak to Him familiarly, and to be His chosen vessel full of the life of God. It is annihilation which causes man no longer to look upon himself or his meanness. By being below all lowliness, he is above all height.

How good it is to be united to such holy souls as these! They obtain for the one person that is joined to them what they themselves possess. Although all the people were united to Moses as children to their father, yet Aaron was bound to him in a special way—they were physical brothers as well as spiritual. There are persons whom God joins after this two-fold manner; and all others, though they may be united to them as their children, still cannot be equal to them in the ministry. There were many priests after the order of Aaron, but Aaron alone went up with Moses; the others dared not even touch the mountain. Yet Aaron was not equal to Moses in everything; he was not raised to the same degree. The communication from God Himself into God Himself in such a sublime a manner was for Moses alone.

20

On Mt. Sinai the Lord gave His commandments to Moses. The people, hearing the thunderings and the trumpet sounds, seeing the burning lights and the mountain covered with smoke, were afraid. They said to Moses, "You speak to us; we will listen. But do not let God speak to us, or we will die." Moses told them not to be afraid, for God had come to test them, so that they would remember their fear of the Lord and refrain from sinning.

God, desiring to submit man to His law, first reminds him of the graces He has bestowed upon him, so that man may not find this law difficult. God desires man to have confidence that this God, who has brought him out of bondage, will not put him anew under the yoke but, on the contrary, He will give *such* a one the necessary grace and strength to keep His divine precepts.

"I will put My Spirit in the midst of you," He says, "and will cause you to walk in My precepts, and keep My statutes, and do good works."

In other words, He Himself will accomplish His law in those who, abandoning themselves completely to Him, allow Him to act in them without resistance.

For this reason His first command is to have no other God before Him — to depend on *no other strength* in order to observe His law, but on His alone. He is a mighty God, who can do everything by His sovereign power. He is also a jealous God. He does not allow man to claim that he can obey God's commandments by his own faithfulness, his own effort, his own industry — by anything, in other words, but God's own strength. As long as we remain in this relationship towards God, robbing Him of nothing that is His, the law becomes easy.

We are not looking upon the law itself (When we do that, we find it very difficult to obey); instead we regard it *in God*, and here it is seen with the *Divine power*, and the Divine life, surmounting every difficulty and living . . . in place of us.

This mighty and jealous God promises to avenge the iniquity of those who hate him. He is not speaking of those who simply violate the law, because such violations are not all intentional. He is speaking of those who *knowingly* turn aside. The ones who turn aside from Him to follow their own ways make themselves the slaves of the law.

These sin against the law itself. They have fallen into a subtle idolatry, attributing *God's strength* to *themselves*. "This is my strength that did this." It isn't. It is the life of God alone which can live out the standard. This idolatry the Lord does not pardon; He judges all *their* works by this law. These persons have made slaves of themselves, for God calls man's sins to account, even to the third and fourth generation. When a man turns to himself for strength, all his works are enslaved.

But in those that love, then love alone is the fulfillment of the law. Upon these God bestows a bountiful grace. The word "grace" here means the pardoning of whatever faults are committed in regard to the law. God does not even look at such faults. When he sees the uprightness of their hearts and the desire they have of pleasing Him, He is content with their love of the law. He does not look at their failure to live the law. He delivers them from its bondage. Therefore, it is said that there is no fear in love, but perfect love casts out fear; for this believer is so engrossed in the love of his God that he can only look upon this same love, and think of nothing else. By the overflow of this Divine love, they forget the law and still they fulfill it perfectly.

To remember God's rest — the Sabbath Day — is to remain in it; and nothing more surely produces holiness than simply resting in God's rest, for it is the repose of God in Himself — of God within the yielded soul, and of the soul in God.

Three kinds of rest are mentioned here.

The first is God resting in the soul which has arrived at union with God's will; God dwells in the soul and rests there. This is what Jesus describes when He says, "If any man love me, he will keep My word, and My Father will love him, and We will come unto him, and make Our abode in him."

The repose of the believer in God can only take place after the resurrection, for it was by the Resurrection he was received into God. Then he finds his perfect rest in Him; his pains and troubles have passed forever. Previously God rested fully in the believer, because he was void of sin, and his will was conformed to God's own; but the believer did not yet find his repose in God, since he walked by a road full of uncertainties, pains, and difficulties. He finds his true rest only when he has entered into God, where he dwells in a tranquil and lasting state, no longer at the mercy of life's changing fortunes.

But the repose of God in Himself is the rest which He enjoys in a soul which is entirely yielded to Him. Here everything of the creature has disappeared; God alone remains. Here God rests — in Himself. He does it not for the sake of the believer, who has entirely passed into God and has no repose different from His. He has reclaimed all that belonged to Him, by the perfect annihilation of the creature. He remains all in all, as Paul put it, and this is the repose of God in God.

Like the Israelites when they saw and heard the awe-inspiring signs of God's presence, the believer who sees God coming near fears death. He knows that to see *Him*, it is necessary to die. From the time when the state of death begins (which lasts for a long period) the believer enters into strange fears, and thinks, "I would rather stop right here than pass through any more unpleasant trials." He keeps himself aloof and desires to protect himself from death. He mistakenly thinks he is approaching God, when in reality he keeps himself at a distance. Deceived by self love, he would rather preserve his own life than allow himself to be carried away by a holy death, which would happily bring him back to life — *in God*.

This leads him to say (more by his resisting actions than by words) to the wiser, more mature Christian who advises him, "Speak to me yourself; for as long as it is only you who speak to me, and I keep to the words of man and human means (or at least what I can understand with my mind), I shall not die. But to go upon the word of God alone, to be led by Him in the obscurity of utter faith—I am afraid He will only lead me into death and loss."

Moses tells the people to "fear not." This pictures the wise counselor who assures those he advises that there is no reason to fear at this time. The time of death has not arrived; this is only a trial which God puts in our lives, to see if we have the courage to enter the way of death.

This people were already well advanced in the interior way, yet they stood afar off; they feared death. But Moses, who had already passed through death and been revived in God, could not die again. Therefore he was not afraid: God was no longer a stranger to him. God and Moses had entered into the common unity of one life, Divine life. God was as much Moses himself as He was God Himself. In this state, what causes death to others gave life to Moses.

Here we see Moses enter into the thick darkness where God is, to teach us that whatever manifestation God chooses in this life, it is always hidden from our understanding. We can have at best only a limited knowledge of it, bounded and covered with the veil of faith.

23

The Lord made precious promises to the Israelites. He said that he would send an angel before them to guard them along the way and to bring them to the promised land. He asked that the people obey this angel and curb their rebellious tendencies. Furthermore, he promised them that the angel would go before them against the alien tribes in the land and destroy them.

God never fails to give us this angel as long as we may need it. This angel is a picture of the ones he graciously gives us as conductors in God's ways. These can guide us only as far as the place prepared for us. After this God alone is our conductor.

The Lord bids us respect these men of wisdom, obey them and not reject them, for His name is in them. In other words, such men represent His person, bear His word, and act on His authority.

24

The people pledged their obedience to their God, and a covenant was made between them, sealed in blood. Moses and seventy elders of Israel climbed Mt. Sinai, beheld God, and ate and drank in His presence.

God called Moses to come alone into the cloud of His glory, and Moses remained there for forty days and forty nights.

No one else had attained to such a sublime state and such a pure love. Moses was as a fountain from which the source was distributed to the rest.

Moses wrote the words of the Lord, in order to leave them to posterity. God causes His servants to write what He has communicated to them of His Divine and hidden truths, so that these truths may remain. In this way many will profit by them.

Moses sent the youngest of the children of Israel to sacrifice peace offerings to the Lord. This is a sacrifice reserved for new believers; their sacrifice is peace and sweetness. It is not the same with advanced believers; they must offer burnt offerings. We know that there are different levels among the children of grace. There are those who have newly come into the spirit and the way, and there are those who have again become children, because they have progressed so far. In the same way Moses distinguishes two sacrifices—the one of peace, suitable for the young children, and the other, of burnt offerings, proper for the more mature.

When Moses read the law, the people immediately and confidently promised to keep it. But he knew them well enough to recognize that in their very certainty was a secret pride. They were relying upon their own strength and were not sufficiently distrustful of their fallen nature. They were not seeking faithfulness from the proper source—the goodness of God.

Moses sprinkled them with the blood that was in the basins. This was a picture of the blood of Jesus Christ, to remind them that the law could not be fulfilled without the strength that was given through His blood. They must be washed and arrayed with this precious blood. Moses' sprinkling of the blood also assured them that every covenant between God and men is established in view of this blood. There is no other basis for a covenant between God and man.

Moses was in God. To the others, however, the

whole mountain appeared covered in darkness. To the outside observer, this state appears terribly dark. So little can be said about it by those who have experienced it that others have difficulty believing what they hear—whatever sign they may have—until they experience it for themselves.

Although Moses had already been intimate with God, conversing with Him in a familiar manner, he still had to wait six days, as if in a purifying period, before entering so near to God. How pure God is! On the seventh day God called to him from the midst of the cloud; and Moses, entering in, was utterly enveloped and stayed there forty days and forty nights. When at last he returned, he was renewed and transformed, bearing the glory of God.

God proceeds by degrees, both in revealing Himself and in bestowing His grace. He extends the creature's capacity little by little, rather than all at once. He does only as much as his child can bear.

Let us look at Moses. He takes no step by himself; he makes no advance by his own movement. He doesn't make a move until God tells him to, yet he promptly does what has been commanded. This is the faithfulness necessary in the utterly passive state, and even more so in annihilation. In this state the interior believer who has died to himself applies himself to everything God desires of him. He does not anticipate his Lord, nor does he resist Him.

25

The Lord here began to instruct Moses in the building of the tabernacle. Here we see the pattern for the ark, the mercy seat with its cherubim, and the lampstand.

This sanctuary, called *the* Tabernacle, represents the center of the soul, even the spirit, the dwelling-place of the Lord. Here the union of God and man takes place; here the Trinity dwells and reveals itself. This spot must be reserved for the Lord. It must be empty of everything else, so that the Lord may dwell and manifest Himself there. This holy place is for Him alone.

The ark was in this sanctuary; from it the oracle of God's word was to issue forth. Until now, God had spoken to His people from a distance, without remaining in a certain place. From this time on He would desire to speak and dwell in the midst of them and to make Himself known and heard in the sanctuary of the center of their souls.

The pure, fine gold of the mercy seat denotes the purity that this center of the soul must possess, so that God may appear and deliver His oracles here. Before serving as the mercy seat, it must be purified by fire from all that is earthy and impure. It must then be tried by the hammer.

The two cherubim which cover the mercy seat are naked *faith*, and total *abandon*. We see here a picture of how faith covers the believer, preventing him from examining himself. *Abandon* protects the believer on another side, preventing him from considering his own loss or advantage—obliging him to blindly abandon himself. But faith and abandon also look upon each other, as do the two cherubim on the cover of the ark. The one cannot exist without the other in a well regulated soul; and faith perfectly responds to abandon, while abandon is submitted to faith.

When the Lord describes meeting with His people and speaking to them from above the mercy seat, He means that from this time on He will make Himself heard from this center of the soul, not from the outer senses.

The pattern that God refers to, which had been shown to Moses on the mountain, is God Himself (in whom exist the eternal ideas of all things) and Jesus Christ, His Word, who expresses these ideas. Everything that is done for the sanctification of souls must be according to this model.

26

On Mt. Sinai, God instructed Moses on how to set up the actual tabernacle, with a veil dividing the sanctuary from the holy of holies.

God desired the sanctuary to be divided from the holy of holies. The sanctuary is the center of the soul, and the holy of holies is God Himself. They are united, yet divided. They are united, in that the center is in God, and God is in the center. Yet they are separated by a difference of state; for to possess God in the center is something very great; but for God to dwell in Himself for Himself—this is a degree still more sublime.

This veil of division between the sanctuary and the holy of holies also represents the substantial distinction which exists eternally between God and His creature, with the inexplicable unity of love and transformation which is wrought by the annihilation of the soul in itself and its reflowing into God. God remains God really distinct from the transformed soul, although the soul—transformed by Divine life and by this ineffable union—becomes one with God.*

* John 17:21; I Cor. 6:17

27

This chapter continues the details which God gave to Moses concerning the building of His tabernacle. God told Moses that Aaron and his sons should prepare lamps and keep them burning from morning to evening before the Lord. This worship should be perpetual among the children of Israel. This lamp can be compared to the lamp of our love for our Lord, which must always burn bright, shining without interruption in His presence.

28

The Lord described to Moses the clothing that Aaron and his sons were to wear when they ministered to Him. In the breastplate of judgment which they would wear, Moses was told to put the Urim and the Thummim. I see the Urim and Thummim as Doctrine and Truth.

Three things may be distinguished in this mysterious thing called the breastplate: judgment, doctrine, and truth. *Judgment* is less sure than doctrine, or teaching, since it depends on the person who judges. (He is applying what he has learned to a particular situation.) *Doctrine* is more dependable than judgment; it is the use of the knowledge and experience by which we judge. But *Truth* is above them all. It is necessary to pass through *judgment* and *doctrine* to enter into truth — the reality of God — which is the source of them both.

Why were these words engraved on the breastplate? To show that our reason is exercised by using our judgment; that judgment submits to, and is instructed by, doctrine; but most of all, that doctrine receives all its light from truth. Judgment is found in us; doctrine is communicated to others to attract their obedience and submission; but truth *dwells in God*. We must be in God to be in truth. For this reason the Holy Spirit is called the Spirit of Truth.

God instructed Moses to make a plate of pure gold and to engrave on it the words, "Holy to the Lord." It was necessary for God's name to be engraved on the forehead, for this name is the all of God.

ALL HOLINESS BELONGS TO HIM WHO IS.

The forehead here represents the supreme part of the soul, where the believer bears this high and holy name of God. Without attaining a most exalted state, the believer can not know the all of God and the nothing of a man in his natural state. Many think they have this knowledge, but they have it only superficially. Annihilation alone can bring experimental conviction of it.

Why does Scripture add, "that they may be accepted before the Lord"? Because God cannot be opposed to a man who rests in the truth of the all of God and his own nothingness. By giving God the justice due Him, he opens himself to God's care and blessings. And it is this truth which he bears symbolically on the breastplate, and in reality upon the forehead.

Man's reason can know the truth of God only in a superficial and figurative way.

God has engraved His truth in the holiest place of the soul. He placed it there at the moment of creation. At man's tragic fall, sin removed it. But Jesus Christ has reestablished — and increased — His truth in souls emptied of self-interest.

29

The Lord told Moses what sacrifices were to be offered, and how. He also speaks of the anointing and preparation of Aaron and his sons as priests.

Both blood and oil were used here to consecrate the priestly garments. The priest, to be consecrated to God, had to be anointed. The oil of the consecration foreshadows the anointing of the Holy Spirit. The blood sprinkled upon those chosen as priests teaches us that they can have no authority except that which is given by Jesus Christ. The blood also signifies that from that time on, whatever was to be accomplished would be accomplished in His blood. All holiness, all priesthood can only be consecrated by the shedding of this blood.

There is something special about the *burnt offering*. All other sacrifices have something of self-interest mixed with them; they are offered either to obtain pardon for sins, or to be delivered from pain, or to appease the wrath of God, or to entreat some grace from His goodness. All such offerings and offer*ers* reserve something to themselves. It is only the *burnt-offering* where *everything* is consumed. It is this perfect sacrifice which represents annihilation and is wholly for God alone. It creates a soothing aroma, a sweet savor, to God.

31

When the Lord had finished speaking with Moses on Mt. Sinai, He gave Moses a written copy of all He had said, on two tablets of stone, written by the very finger of God.

With His finger God engraves His law upon stone; He does this when the believer has arrived at the state of utter rest in God. At this point the believer has no other law than the one written on his heart. The law of God has become natural to him. The soul, like the stone, receives the law written with the finger of God.

Now it is up to God Himself to fulfill His law in this saint, at His pleasure. Here is a saint immersed in pure love; and love is the perfection of the law (Matthew 22:40). So, at this stage, the saint exists in the perfection of the law, and in its true fulfillment. The believer, perfectly submitted to God, does not have to think about the law. He simply follows it faithfully in every point. He is united to the will of God, and transformed *into that very will*, surpassing every law, by God's all-encompassing love.

32

When Moses was delayed on the mountain, the Israelites asked Aaron to make them idols to lead them.

The Israelites represent the man who is abandoned to God and already far advanced in His ways. Yet we see that this man can still sin in one all-important area: idolatry. I may be criticized by learned men for making such a statement; therefore I will explain it at greater length.

Idolatry can be committed in *more* than one way. There is only one being who deserves worship, and that is the one true God. Thus men commit idolatry when they worship some created person or thing as God, or when they believe in more than one god. (That is the same as believing in no god at all!)

There is another more subtle, hidden form of idolatry. We worship God, but at the same time we give *some* of the worship, honor and trust due to God to some created thing or things. When we wrong the one true God in this way we are really worshipping idols as surely as the Israelites were.

For instance, Paul says that there are those

who make a god of their belly; that is idolatry. There are many similar forms of self-interest, in which we love something of this creation more than we love God. We may not even be aware of it, but we are really worshipping possessions, or success, or pleasure, and thus robbing God of some of the worship He deserves.

We see the Israelites, here, falling into this form of idolatry. They love God, but their love is mixed with self-interest. They have made great progress in the way of the spirit, giving themselves totally to the Lord. But now they relapse into themselves; in so doing they open themselves up to a great fall.

Up until now, God did not judge too severely the many weaknesses of this people. All their murmurings and complaints were graciously overlooked. God continued to bless them.

But now the people commit *idolatry*; they have *abandoned* their inward walk with their God. This time they will not be able to return except by a miracle of mercy. This idolatry is committed when we withdraw our will from its union with God; we choose to depend once again on our own strength. We tire of depending on God; we depart from our destitution and loss in God. We try to find, in our own power and activity, what can *only* be found in God.

In the shameful story of the golden calf we see a picture of the unfaithful believer withdrawing from God and foolishly relying on his own efforts to obtain the grace he had received from God. The man in this story now claims that he has escaped captivity by his own means! Hence, he adds the sin of blasphemy to that of idolatry!

We worship God both with our mind and our heart. We worship God with our mind by acknowledging that God alone is supreme. The first step toward idolatry comes when the believer withdraws his *mind* from the worship owed to God alone, and recognizes *any* sovereign power other than God. The worship of the *heart* is the love we have for God. Thus when a man loves anything more than God, he commits idolatry in the heart.

Your proper state is one of constant, *secret* adoration of your God, acknowledging His supreme power, His sovereignty in everything which happens in your life, letting yourself be conducted by Him without worrying about the consequences. We trust God to take care of everything, realizing that we are bound to fail if we depend on our own strength. To withdraw from this state is to commit idolatry of the *spirit*.

As I have said, the Israelites at the base of Mt.

Sinai represent an advanced stage in the believer's walk. The believer, developed to this point, cannot sin except in this matter of idolatry.

You see, as long as the spirit does not issue from its rest, nor the will from its union with God's perfect will, the believer cannot sin in spite of his own weaknesses. The two states — (1) *rest in God's will* and (2) *sin* — are incompatible. If I sin, I cease immediately to be united to the will of God. And if I am united to the will of God, I am not in an active state of sinning.

John expressed this truth when he wrote (I John 5:18), "We know that whoever is born of God cannot sin; but the birth which he has from God keeps him, and the evil one does not touch him." To be born of God is to remain united to Him in mind and heart by a perfect abandon. So long as man is in this center of Safety, neither sin nor the wicked one can touch him. But as soon as he comes out of this state through self-interest, he is pierced by the arrows of sin and the wicked one.

All persons of experience will understand me.

Notice that when God sends Moses down to deal with the sinning Israelites, He calls the people *Moses' people*, and not *His* own, as before. This is on account of their sin. As soon as this people had begun to commit idolatry they became like animals; they were changed entirely. And, losing all intelligence, they provoked God's wrath.

Moses, being innocent, places himself between God and the people as a barrier, to prevent the torrent of His wrath from bursting upon them. Here we see a surprising thing. The man who is emptied of himself has a power with God — even a power to influence God. And God acts on his behalf, even in matters of great importance.

God almost seems to entreat Moses. "Let me alone," He says. The man who is the friend of God prevents His anger from kindling, as if God were not almighty; for a man who has given up his own life, and possesses only God, has power over Him in some way. The Lord was truly then . . . the God of Moses. Moses pleads with him, "Lord, why is Your anger kindled against Your people?" He reminds God that they *are* His people, and not Moses'; and he reminds Him of the great blessings He has bestowed upon them. He prays that all that God has done for them thus far may not be in vain.

Moses here entreats the Lord not to destroy the Israelites, because the Egyptians can then say, "With evil intent He brought them out to kill them in the mountains and to destroy them from the face of the earth."

Like Moses, mature men of God, viewing the falling away of younger saints, pray fervently to God not to reject His people on account of their sins.

One of their concerns is that this internal walk with the Lord will be discredited by its critics if those who begin such a walk end up perishing. These critics will say, "It is not good to trust ones-self wholly to God; it can be carried to excess. It is much better to trust one's own efforts."

Perhaps the people who make such statements should look around them and see the state of the people who trust in their own efforts!

Moses also reminds God of the faithfulness of His promises. God had sworn that if any followed the road of pure faith, they would arrive at the Promised Land, which is union with God and His true and real possession. How good God is, to hold back His just vengeance at the mere word of one of His servants who is without self-interest and is only concerned for God's glory! Moses does not complain of the trouble this people cause Moses. He does not mention the grief which *he* would suffer if he were to see them perish. Moses is not concerned with what would be said of him, nor of all that he might be accused of. His only fear is that God may be blamed and discredited. Oh, how admirable is a man without self-interest!

The expression "reduced to nakedness" in v. 25 ["out of control" NAS] well describes the state of this fallen people. They had already given up their own strength when they agreed to be conducted into God, so that they might be clothed with God's own strength. So now when they sin, they are doubly stripped. They lose God's strength by their sin; now they no longer find any of their own to fall back on.

It is difficult for these persons to return to the inward way once again. According to the author of Hebrews (Hebrews 6:4-6), "It is almost impossible for those who have been once enlightened, who have tasted the gift of heaven and have received the Holy Spirit, to be renewed again by repentance after once falling." They can still be saved, but it is very difficult for them to regain the degree from which they have fallen. The manner in which they must repent is very different from that necessary for other sinners who are not advanced in the ways of the Spirit.

Now, without God's strength *or* their own, they are placed completely naked in the hands of their enemies. These enemies could not harm the interior believer while he remained in God as in a fortress. But now that they find the believer defenseless, these same enemies delight in taking vengeance. Moses called out from the gate of the camp, "Whoever is for the Lord, come to me!" And it was the Levites who responded to his call. Moses wants to find those who, in the midst of corporate sin, have not allowed themselves to be corrupted by the general idolatry. He calls upon them to join him; and the whole tribe of Levi, who will later constitute the priesthood, obey him. These priests of the Most High, who represent believers of pure sacrifice, *remain* in their sacrifice, and do not leave it, even when all those around them have fallen. By the Levites' rare faithfulness, they earn the right to join Moses in the office of the priesthood.

But look at the cost of the Levites' faithfulness! They are commanded to kill whoever could lead them to commit idolatry in the future — even brothers, friends, or dear ones. By this act the faithful Levites show the other survivors what true repentance is.

Such a knowledge, causing the onlookers to despair, leads them once again to thoroughly distrust themselves, and to lose themselves in God. Without looking back at their fall, however glaring and enormous, they must give themselves to God, to serve His will eternally. They now see clearly their powerlessness.

At this point, putting to death all their own strength, the repentant believers rid themselves without pity of the self-love and self-interest which caused their idolatry. In essence they become the instrument of destruction upon self-love and self-interest. By a new and pure sacrifice, they place in God's hands the pardon of their fault, abandoning it to His will — whatever will give Him the most glory. They do not claim — do not even desire — to be assured of His mercy.

In v. 28 and 29, we see the Levites carrying out the word of Moses. Three thousand men fell before their swords that day.

Believers who actively fall . . . must then give themselves to the mercy of God. Their trust in His mercy enables them to repent and obtain pardon for their sin. But those who have come this far must act without self-interest, in order to rise again by repentance and come out of their fall better off than before — strengthened in love. They must offer themselves up to the Divine justice, willing to accept the punishment they deserve. See them throw themselves upon the mercy of God's great love, not asking for pardon of their sins, but only for His will and greatest glory. And His love covers in one moment a multitude of the greatest sins. Thus they sacrifice without mercy all self-interest (here pictured in the son, the brother, and the friend).

This kind of repentance, the repentance of the interior believer, has the power of returning the soul to the state from which it has fallen. Any other kind of repentance might, indeed, assure his salvation, but *never* re-establish him in the state from which he has fallen. On the contrary, other forms of repentance might even remove him further from that state, causing the believer to enter all the more deeply into his self-interest.

This manner of repentance, after the fall of such believers, is difficult. It is extremely painful to self-love, still living in them. In fact these believers imagine that they would rather be flayed alive than simply rest, drinking in the penalty of their fault, and allowing themselves to be devoured by the burning heat of confusion. Nevertheless, the more annihilating such repentance is for man, the more glorious for God. And such repentance is so pure that the believer has no sooner returned to it, than he is re-established in the state from which he fell. Furthermore, he is Re-established with advantages which he did not have before.

This repentance which is mentioned in Ecc. 10:4:

> If the spirit of the ruler rises against you, do not leave your place; for the remedies that will be applied unto you will heal you of the greatest sins.

The place of each believer is where God had set that believer before his fall. (However miserably we may have fallen, we must not leave this place.) A devotee of Christ must simply return to this place and continue his course, trusting that, if he peacefully remains in his abjection — yielded to all of God's plans for him — God will apply upon him the most sovereign remedies. By these remedies the believer will be healed of his sins, with even an increase of blessings.

Because what I am saying is so important, you who are spiritual directors need to understand this counsel, so that, *instead* of being *astonished* at the falls of *advanced* believers, you may sustain them in their desolation: give them new courage, cause them to hope for a happy return to God. Encourage them to be faithful . . . not to willfully return to their former practices, but to love even their present state of confusion so that they may exalt God's glory all the more. In this way the believer makes a peaceful and passive repentance in the very place of the interior way from which he has fallen.

David's repentance was of this kind. His repentance was well accepted by the Lord, as we see; after David's fall and repentance, the Holy Spirit continued to speak through David's mouth, and dictate to him the psalms, just as he had before his sin.

Notice also the repentance of Peter. Peter denied his Lord, yet he did not renounce by his fall the commission which he had received from Jesus Christ. (Jesus Christ had elected him first among the apostles.) Instead, Peter could be found exercising his gift a few days after with divine courage.

Neither of these great men left the rank which God had given them in His church, despite their sin. This teaches us that it is not necessary, no matter what our offense, to leave the degree of the interior life to which we have attained, since the Divine Physician has remedies for all our evils and states. Far from wishing us to turn back, under pretext of starting over again by another road, Your Lord desires you to double your pace, and to give Him your hand in perfect trust and total abandon. By doing this you will advance still further.

Although sin is the greatest of all evils, God is able to use even sin in perfecting us.

By the confusion sin causes us, and by the experience it gives us of our weakness, sin delivers us (by crushing our own self-existence and self-love) from these great obstacles to our annihilation, and from our flowing into God. God has permitted such falls in many of His saints so that He may conduct them afterwards, even more swiftly and surely, into Himself alone.

The repentance of spiritual persons who have fallen is often so very grievous because their fall takes away *assurance* rather than giving assurance. Consequently few are faithful enough to remain in such a state of uncertainty. As a result there are few who, after such falls, are re-established in their state. But if you find yourself in this perilous a position, be firm and constant to bear the weight of this yoke. Do not wish to be relieved *by your own efforts*. Find His! What an advantage you will then gain! And what glory for God!

In verse 30 we hear Moses say to the people, "You have committed a great sin; and now I am going up to the Lord; perhaps I can make atonement for your sin."

The character of a true shepherd is unselfish love. Moses—and any good shepherd—begins by reproving the people for their sin and making that sin known to them. Then he pleads with God to pardon them, offering to bear, himself, the penalty they deserve for their great crime.

Oh how admirable is this speech! "Lord," he

said, "either pardon this people, or blot me out of Your book which You have written." The book he refers to is the *Book of Life*, in which Moses knew his name was recorded. *This* kind of praying forces God to pardon; such a pure and disinterested love obtains all things. Paul, the great conductor of souls, prayed the same sort of prayer when he desired to be accursed for the salvation of his brethren. Both Moses and Paul knew from experience how much the sacrifice of a perfect love could accomplish.

33

The Lord said to Moses, "Depart, go up from here, you and the people whom you have brought up from the land of Egypt, to the land of which I swore to Abraham, Isaac, and Jacob, saying, 'To your descendants I will give it.'"

You are willing, Lord, in spite of sin, to reward this ungrateful and unfaithful people. You do this because of the faithfulness of Your word, and You do it on behalf of the faith, sacrifice, and abandon which they formerly practiced. But permit me to say to You, that these very rewards are terrible punishments, since whatever is agreeable to the senses must hurt the spirit.

God continued, "And I will send an angel before you. . . . Go up to a land flowing with milk and honey; for I will not go up in your midst, because you are an obstinate [stiff-necked] people, lest I destroy you on the way."

We see that the Lord is willing to give His people blessings, consolations, and miracles, such as visible angels to accompany them in their way of light. An ignorant man may esteem these great things highly; but he does not see the horrible punishment contained in these things. The punishment is unique. God loads them with His gifts and thereby deprives them of Himself.

What a horrible threat! What a terrible state. Yet, one known by *too many*!

Take away all the rest, Lord, and give us Yourself. That is sufficient.

This is, then, the punishment with which God smites an ungrateful, carnal, and self-interested people.

Notice that these words, "For I will not go up with you," express how God grants His gifts in place of Himself. Very often people see such a "blessing" as a reward when it is really a punishment.

The Lord goes on to say that it is because of their obstinacy that He will not go with them; He would be obliged to consume and annihilate them, if He continued with them . . . for He is determined to conduct them in the pure and naked way if He goes with them. This is the way by which we can proceed perfectly to God, and He had seen that they were *incapable* of this trial. Destruction would be the inevitable outcome.

The people of Israel mourned when they heard the words of the Lord, and they did not put on their ornaments.

The crime of the people had not altogether robbed them of the remembrance of the truth, and they acted with great wisdom. They mourned at the Lord's decision. They set no value on all the Lord's gifts, and they stripped themselves of their ornaments, to show God that they wished to be stripped of all goods, in order to have the happiness of possessing Him in their midst. This is a proper way of acting, to win God.

God wished to test this people, to see if they really longed for Him, or only His gifts. He threatened them with Himself in a terrible manner: "Should I go up in your midst for even one moment," He said, "I would destroy you. Now, therefore, put off your ornaments (all that remains of My favors) from you, that I may know what I will do with you."

There are many of us who, on a similar occasion, would say: "Let the *angel* guide us, and let us keep His gifts! It is all right if God does not come with us."

This is, to a large degree, the present state of the church.

But this well-instructed people, on this occasion, do quite the opposite. By their silence they show that, although it costs them something, they prefer God to everything else; they strip themselves immediately of all their ornaments.

But why does Scripture first say that they had

not put on their customary ornaments, and now say that they stripped themselves of their ornaments? This is the way I understand it. They do not put on the graces God would give them in place of Himself; on the contrary, they despise them. And to show Him still further that it is He Himself they desire and not His gifts, they strip themselves even of the gifts that remain to them, which they had previously received. They prefer annihilation to everything else, if only God will lead them.

They had no sooner accomplished this generous stripping than Moses set up before them the tabernacle of the covenant, as if to assure them that God would Himself accompany them. As soon as Moses had entered into the tabernacle the Lord Himself appeared there, and spoke in the cloud as before.

At the tabernacle these poor criminals found their refuge; there they asked God for all that they needed. They knew by the pillar of cloud that God was with them, and immediately they worshipped from their tents—that is, from the place of their repose. The utterly yielded one knows how to worship in everything he does without leaving his repose. This manner of worshipping is more perfect than any other.

The people worshipped from afar, and standing; for the perfect worship, made in spirit and truth by faith and love, penetrates all distance and does not depend on any certain condition or position of the body. Worship and worshipers rise to God. Yet even though this repentant people's worship was far advanced, it did not approach that of Moses.

This chosen and unique friend of God speaks to God face to face, in the most intimate of all unions, elevated above the human faculties. For the sake of friendship, God has raised this man's capacity and lowered Himself. God and a man now speak face to face. God treats His friend in so familiar a manner that it may be compared to the way *we* act with *our* most intimate friends. God conceals nothing from him.

When Moses returned to the camp, Joshua would not leave the tabernacle. It is the custom of young saints, just entering into the interior way, to remain continually in prayer; they are so charmed with the presence of God that they cannot pull themselves away. A sweet and penetrating love, seizing hold of these ardent young believers, keeps them buried in themselves. The strong and living presence of God which fills them, concentrates them so sweetly within themselves (as in a tabernacle) that they do not want to leave.

The wise director, following Moses' example,

leaves them to their prayer, for the time has not yet come to draw them out.

Moses now prayed to see the Lord's face, to know Him, and to find favor in His sight; and he prayed that the Lord would look favorably on His people.

This prayer of Moses may appear bold, insulting to God . . . and furthermore, utterly useless! True, Moses' prayer could be called bold; for what mortal man ought to aspire to a clear vision of God? Such a prayer could be called insulting to God, since the one who prays assumes that God reveals His countenance (though some say that God does no such thing *in this life*). And finally, this prayer could be called useless, since Scripture says that God had spoken to Moses face to face already. But Moses' prayer is none of these.

Moses' request was a just one on this occasion, for he was not acting on his own behalf, but for a great nation of interior people. Moses really wants to know (as do his people) if God Himself rather than His angel will lead them. They are looking for reassurance that God alone will be their conductor into Himself by the frightening road which they still have to travel. (This road is becoming more dangerous the nearer it is to the end.)

Moses desired to see if God would lead this people. He wanted to know if Israel had been re-established in grace; and he wished to judge how safe the road was which they were going to take. Moses must also see God's face — have the clear sight and understanding of the words spoken to him — so that he can teach those words without error.

It is remarkable that a believer may already enjoy and understand something himself, and yet still be in need of the light and ease of expression to make others understand it. Paul has distinguished two different gifts: the gift of speaking in different tongues, and the gift of interpreting those tongues. And among the gifts of the Holy Spirit, there is a great difference between *wisdom*, *understanding*, and *counsel*.

Wisdom is the discernment of Divine truths by tasting of them *in experience*. *Understanding* allows them to be thoroughly grasped. But *counsel* is the ability to express the Divine truths clearly *to others*. For this same reason Paul said that the countenance of God had been revealed to him; "for us," he said, "in whom the open countenance of the Lord expresses his glory as in a mirror."

We see again that Moses was not thinking of himself as he prayed, when he adds, "Look favorably upon Your people; for it is on their behalf that I make this request."

God continues to assure Moses that he has God's special protection. He promises Moses a place of rest. In other words, Moses himself will always find God, will always have rest in Him; he need not trouble himself about other things.

But the great heart of Moses, forgetting all self-interest and thinking only of his flock, refuses this advantage. He continues to entreat his God. Moses protests that if he does not see God going before his people, he cannot allow them to depart from this place.

Moses asked the Lord, "How shall we know, I and Thy people, that we have found grace before You, if You do not go with us, that we may be in glory and honor among all peoples that dwell on the earth?"

> What hope will we have of pardon? How shall we have victory over our enemies? How can we walk in safety if You Yourself do not come with us?

Such a follower of the Lord prefers to lose all, rather than to lose his God! How safe we are when we walk under God's leadership! But if we walk any other way, we are exposed to infinite dangers.

God grants Moses what he asks, for He knows him by his name: true and legitimate shepherd, full of unselfish love. On account of Moses' pure and passionate love, God cannot refuse him anything. This is what God calls "finding grace in His sight." At this time, however, He only grants Moses victory over his enemies. This is not to say that He will *not* grant him the rest; but He is pleased to make him wait and long for such a wonderful prize, which is worth suffering to gain, and is worth seeking after with a burning desire.

Such a man is not content with an earthly or limited reward. Moses again begs for the same favor, though he expresses himself differently. "Show me Your glory," he says, as if to say, I will not be content until I see Your glory, and what You are in Yourself. God promises Moses that He will show him all His goodness. Actually He Himself is the highest good, and the center of all that is good.

God's answer, however, seems to find fault with Moses for making such ardent requests. He says to him: "I will be gracious unto whom I will be gracious, and I will show mercy unto whom I will show mercy." But, Moses, do not let this apparent harshness turn you away. This will actually be a greater good for you than all the preceding caresses. It is, indeed, a sign that the Lord, out of His great love for you, will grant you all that you desire.

When God promises His blessings to His servants, He bestows those blessings with a thousand signs of affection; *but* . . . He grants the greatest good in seeming to repel. When God outwardly rejects, it is to introduce inwardly. For example, when Jesus Christ refuses the Canaanite woman, He does so only to hear her with more compassion.

The natural man must be destroyed in himself before he can be received into God. He must know that he can look only to the pure goodness of God for this ineffable grace. As Paul puts it (in explaining this very verse), "It is not of him that wills, nor of him that runs, but of God who shows mercy."

God says to Moses that he cannot see His face, for no man can see Him and live.

God refuses Moses' request. In doing so He instructs him in the attitude necessary for the full enjoyment of God. No one can see God who is not truly dead to all self-life—in fact, to all that is not God. Thus He does not say, "No one shall see Me without dying," but "no one shall see Me and live." He wants us to understand that to arrive at this supreme joy, one death alone is not sufficient—nor even several. There must not remain the smallest particle of self-life at all.

There are several spiritual deaths, all necessary for the soul's purification—that of the senses, the faculties, and the center. Each of these deaths is accomplished only by the loss of *many* lives; because there are *many* natural attachments and supports which sustain a man's self-life. In order to see God, to be united to Him by the most intimate union . . . the believer absolutely must be deprived of *all* these lives. If the holy flame of pure love does not annihilate our natural attachments and supports in this earthly realm, the purifying fire must devour them in the spiritual realm.

The Lord then offers to place Moses in a rock, where he can see God from the back, after He has passed by.

This place in which to enjoy God is near Him; more than that, this holy place is in Himself . . . and *is* Himself. In order to possess this priceless treasure, we must be established upon the rock of God's immovable nature. "When," says the Lord, "My glory shall pass by, I will cover you with the hand of My protection, so that you may be able to bear such a great favor as this, which otherwise would consume you. Nevertheless, you shall only see Me as through a narrow opening, or the cleft in a rock" . . . (which is the most subtle point of the Spirit).

"When this majestic state of My glory, which

can only be seen in this life as a flash of lightning, shall have passed, I shall withdraw My hand, which protected you from seeing My glory (lest your soul should be separated from your body; for your natural frame is too feeble to bear the weight of such glory). Then you will see Me! Then you will comprehend in some manner, by the glimpse of My Divinity which I will give you, that I AM THAT I AM, and that in Me is . . . *all.*"

Moses was allowed to see God from the back side. Moses will see only what can be comprehended by man — even man raised up to his most exalted state. Even in an elevated state, you can perceive only the surface of what God is.

34

God now tells Moses to cut out two stone tablets like the ones that were broken, so that He can again write on them.

God looks upon Moses with singular kindness in allowing Himself to be seen by him; but it is on condition that His law be engraved upon tablets of stone that *will not be broken again*. God shows here that He desires to engrave His law upon hearts which, by their steadfastness, are placed beyond the reach of unfaithfulness.

Moses, when he has the happiness of beholding God upon the mountain, expresses the joy of a man who receives such a gift. His words point out to us how those who are visited by God in their interior center, feeling these delicious touches, can only allow the fire of their love (with which they are kindled) to evaporate by a thousand praises which they offer to their God. Here is a picture of the bride receiving her clearest knowledge of her Lord. He reveals Himself to her. She calls Him Lord, God, true, merciful, long suffering. She cannot praise highly enough His Divine qualities; she loves them all equally, His justice as well as His mercy, His power as well as His virtue. Because she gazes at Him without self-interest, she is enraptured that these are the perfections of her God shining forth in Himself, or on behalf of His children.

Moses uses this moment of blessing to obtain what he desires. He worships God first; then he entreats Him to lead His people, so that, as Moses says, "You may pardon us and may possess us." The surest mark of pardon for sins is to be possessed by God and to possess Him within one's self because God cannot dwell where sin exists. As God pardons sins, He must re-enter into possession of the heart and re-establish it in Him as it was before its death in sin.

God promises Moses what he desires. He also assures Moses that God has even greater blessings for him than anything he has received up till now. When God desires to dwell within our spirits, we must be stripped, by God's working in us, of all that we possess. But when God, who is the source of all blessings, takes up His abode with us, He brings with Him blessings unlike any we have ever experienced. Such gifts, like the ornaments of His inner court, cannot exist without *Him.*

God admonishes Moses not to make a covenant of friendship with the inhabitants of the land they are about to enter. God likewise counsels the ones who seek Him to have nothing more to do with those who are living in and for themselves. There is a danger here to believers that they may be drawn out of their state of loss in God, that they may follow the example of these unworthy companions and return to themselves. This would bring about their ruin.

Again God commands the Israelites to worship no other God, as they have so recently done; for His Name is *The Jealous God.*

> Oh my God, What a holy jealousy You have for the heart and spirit of Your creatures! You want them to belong to You alone and to never again allow themselves to be seduced by any idolatry.

In v. 16 we see God warn the Israelites against intermarrying with the peoples they will find in the Promised Land — and with good reason. God uses intermarriage to represent idolatry; he even calls idolatry fornication. Just as God's people must belong to God alone, we, as His people, must give our hearts to Him alone. As soon as we withdraw our hearts from Him and offer them to something else, we commit adultery. James is talking about the same thing when he exclaims, "You adulteresses, do you not know that friendship with the world is hostility toward God? Therefore, whoever wishes to be a friend of the world makes himself an enemy of God" (James 4:4).

When Moses came down from the mountain, the brilliance of his face was a visible sign of his flowing into, and sublime transformation in, God Himself. The fulness of this experience overflowed even into his physical appearance.

Wisely, Moses, who had unveiled his face before the Lord, covered his face again when speaking to the people. His conduct here is an example for us, to show us that persons of this degree should not talk about the secrets revealed to them, nor what they experience, to others who have not had similar experiences. Such knowledge would only frighten and repulse believers who are not ready to understand. These secrets should be known only to God and to those to whom He has revealed them, or to those who are ready to receive them. With others, everything is covered with a veil, unperceived by their spirit (however perceptive they believe themselves to be). If this veil were lifted, they could not bear the splendor that would shine forth from a person who has been immersed in God's glory.

35

The Lord commanded the Israelites to kindle no fires in their dwellings on the Sabbath Day. This commandment speaks of the rest to be enjoyed by those who have entered into God's day of rest. They must do nothing of themselves, but remain simply as they are, kept by God.

To kindle fire means to stir up a little affection, to keep warm the feeling of God's love. This is permitted to those who have not reached this utter rest in God. With them it is still necessary to remain active and to sustain themselves by some sign; but this must no longer be done on the Sabbath Day (in the state of repose in God). At this point, to do so would violate the holiness of the sabbath, interrupting God's rest.

You who are called to this holy rest, enter in, and remain there without fear. Respect the majesty of God, who desires to be perfectly worshipped in you by silence and repose. Remember that this is the sabbath that remains to us in the law of grace, as Paul says in Hebrews 4:9. Once you, the most chosen people of God, have been introduced to this sabbath, continue to celebrate it. Even death will not separate you from this state, for the sabbath of God is eternal.

Now the Lord asks that the people make a contribution to Him; and He asks them to give with a willing heart. These first offerings that God demands are the first good works. This is the beginning of the spiritual life which, newly born to God's love, we can consecrate to Him, since we can act of ourselves. All our actions must be referred to God, without retaining anything whatever for ourselves. By this voluntary offering of all that lies in our power, God sanctifies and consecrates to Himself all the rest, because we have made Him a free gift of our will. He so totally possesses our whole self that, from now on, He deals with us as a King with His willing subjects.

This is the most certain and the shortest way (perhaps I should say the *only* way) of acquiring perfection: to abandon your heart to the power of God, that He may do with that heart as He pleases. A person generous enough to do this, has gotten rid of himself. And in getting rid of himself, he has shaken off the greatest enemy of his perfection! Now that he is happily placed within the hands of God, he has lost all power over himself.

But he has lost his power only by giving it voluntarily to God. They could not make a more holy, just, or advantageous use of his liberty than to return it and consecrate it to his God (who was the one who gave him liberty in the first place). This is not to say that he can not claim back his liberty through unfaithfulness. There are very few who make a perfect gift of it. Most hold back something in reserve.

But if this perfect sacrifice were made all at once, we would be perfect in that very instant; the truth is that no imperfection can remain where God's will acts and reigns without resistance.

These material offerings are a picture of the spiritual sacrifices God desires of us; and utterly happy are those who offer such sacrifices gladly and with understanding.

It is necessary only to offer to the Lord these first fruits of our will and the free right we have over ourselves, in order for Him to perform in us the work of the tabernacle. God, by means of Moses, in this desert (and in the rest that His people take there), instructs all spiritual persons in the way they ought to take to succeed in the work of their Christian maturity; and whoever has enough understanding to penetrate through those shadows will see this way with delight.

The tabernacle is the dwelling place of God. It is He Himself who builds this dwelling place within us, as soon as we have yielded Him our rights. We need only turn away from what is

151

created, by a gentle yet firm control of our thoughts and hearts. We turn away from what is created, to live solely with God in the midst of ourselves. We need only rise above our own frailty and plunge into God, to find there all that we need. *Then* God begins to perform His work in us.

He is bountiful! He makes use of everything in order to construct His interior palace. He makes *everything* work for good to those that love Him and are called to holiness according to His purpose (Romans 8:28). He even uses the evil intentions of all who oppose us. These evil intentions serve as strokes of a hammer, to polish the outside of God's building by the suffering they cause us. In the meantime God Himself works within and builds His tabernacle there.

In order for this to take place, I repeat: Everything must be offered *freely* and with *open heart*. Scripture says that the Israelites all gave willingly. This shows that God never violates our freedom. In dealing with us He uses love, so that we freely give Him what we have to offer.

36

The best things have their times and seasons for completion. Can there by anything better than offering to God what one possesses? Why then does Scripture say, in v. 5, that the Israelites offer here *more* than is necessary? The reason is that once we have freely offered our liberty to God, there is no more necessity to offer it; it is no longer ours! We would be obliged to take back the gift in order to give it again.

You may say, however, that we can always offer new virtues. It is true that we can always offer new fruits — as long as we possess the tree. But when we have given up the root, it would be ridiculous to still wish to offer the tree's fruits. Obviously the fruits now belong to the owner of the root, and we cannot desire to give them again without taking back our claim to ownership.

It is common, however, for young believers to keep offering themselves to the Lord. There are many reasons a young believer may do this: Perhaps the gift was not made in all its perfection from the beginning. Perhaps the believer desires to renew his commitment after having withdrawn that commitment through unfaithfulness. Sometimes the repeated gift is simply an outpouring of love from a full heart, which takes pleasure in confirming all the believer has done for his God. And finally, God Himself, who loves to see this sacrifice of love many times renewed, may have asked the believer for this assurance of his gift.

Moses ordered a proclamation throughout the camp that there should be no more offerings, because enough had been gathered for the purpose at hand. In fact, there was even more than was needed.

Moses, a wise leader and well instructed in the ways of God, forbids either men (symbolizing Christ) or women (representing the Church) to offer any more gifts. The offering that has been made of the self is enough to allow God to act, and to build His sanctuary Himself, according to His eternal design.

They have already exceeded the command that God had given. The love of self-activity often leads us to give ourselves when — actually — we ought not to do so any longer. This "re-giving" would always occur if those who lead did not warn us against it, with patience and firmness; or if God (making use of the right He has acquired over us by our free gift) did not render us powerless to do so, by weakening our abilities and sapping our strength.

40

As soon as the tabernacle is finished, according to God's order, He immediately comes to fill it with His presence, with visible signs that His Majesty resides there. In the same way, as soon as our interior has been prepared as God desires, He comes to dwell there. He comes *cloaked*, so that only through faith can we recognize Him. Although this cloud is not God, He is *within* the cloud.

When this interior tabernacle, or the center of the soul, is filled with God Himself, nothing else can enter — not even things that seem very, very holy. Everything which is of God resolves itself into God as He draws near, and cannot be distinguished; and all that is not of God remains outside.

The inner sanctuary must be entirely empty, so that the Majesty of God may come to dwell within you. May God so find you in that Day.

END

BOOKS BY MADAME GUYON

EXPERIENCING THE DEPTHS OF JESUS CHRIST

Guyon's first and best known book. One of the most influential pieces of Christian literature ever penned on the deeper Christian life. Among the multitudes of people who have read this book and urged others to read it are: John Wesley, Adoniram Judson, Watchman Nee, Jesse Penn-Lewis, Zinzendorf, and the Quakers. A timeless piece of literature that has been on the "must read" list of Christians for 300 years.

THE STORY OF MADAME GUYON'S LIFE, by T.C. Upham

If you enjoy reading Jeanne Guyon's writings, you will wish to read the story of her life. Through the centuries a multitude of Christians have held it to be the most outstanding life story of any Christian woman in church history. Truly one of Christendom's best known and most frequently read biographies.

Her well-known autobiography details her life only to about 40, whereas she became an internationally known figure and spiritual influence in Europe after that time. Some of the most significant aspects of her life story are not included in her remarkable autobiography. T.C. Upham's history of her life, on the other hand, recounts her fame in the Court of Louis XIV, her clash with Bossuet, her trial, the international storm created by Fenelon's clash with Bossuet over her teachings, her imprisonment in the dungeon of Vincennes, her four years as a prisoner in the infamous Bastille.

One of the half dozen truly great Christian biographies.

THE SPIRITUAL ADVENTURE

This book could well be called volume two of EXPERIENCING THE DEPTHS OF JESUS CHRIST. Here is a look at the experiences a more advanced and faithful Christian might encounter in his/her walk with the Lord. Without question, next to EXPERIENCING THE DEPTHS, here is Mme. Jeanne Guyon's best book.

UNION WITH GOD

Written as a companion book to EXPERIENCING THE DEPTHS OF JESUS CHRIST, and includes 22 of her poems.

SONG OF SONGS
GENESIS

Jeanne Guyon wrote a commentary on the Bible; here are two of those books. SONG OF SONGS has been popular through the centuries and has greatly influenced several other well-known commentaries on the Song of Songs.

THE SPIRITUAL LETTERS OF MADAME GUYON

Here is spiritual counseling at its very best. There is a Christ-centeredness to Jeanne Guyon's counsel that is rarely, if ever, seen in Christian literature.

THE WAY OUT

A spiritual study of Exodus as seen from "the interior way."

THE BOOK OF JOB

Guyon looks at the life of Job from the view of the deeper Christian life.

CHRIST OUR REVELATION

A profound and spiritual look at the book of Revelation.

CLASSICS ON THE DEEPER CHRISTIAN LIFE

PRACTICING HIS PRESENCE

The monumental seventeenth century classic by Brother Lawrence, now in modern English. One of the most read and recommended Christian books of the last 300 years.

The twentieth century missionary, Frank Laubach, while living in the Philippines, sought to put into practice Brother Lawrence's words. Included in this edition are excerpts from Frank Laubach's diary. This book is a Christian classic by *any* standard; this book consistently shows up on more "top-ten must-read" book recommendation lists than any other piece of Christian literature in print.

THE SPIRITUAL GUIDE

At the time Jeanne Guyon was teaching in the royal court of Louis XIV (in France), a man named Michael Molinos was leading a spiritual revival among the clergy and laymen of Rome! He actually lived in the Vatican, his influence reaching to all Italy and beyond. The great, the near great, the unknown sought him out for spiritual counsel. He was the spiritual director of many of the illuminaries of the seventeenth century. He wrote THE SPIRITUAL GUIDE to meet the need of a growing hunger for spiritual direction. The book was, for a time, probably the most popular book in Europe, but was later banned and condemned to be burned. The author was convicted and sentenced to a dungeon after one of the most sensational trials in European history.

Here, in modern English, is that remarkable book.

CHURCH HISTORY

These two books bring to bear a whole new perspective on church life.

THE EARLY CHURCH

This book tells, in a "you are there" approach, what it was like to be a Christian in the first century church, recounting the events from Pentecost to Antioch. By Gene Edwards.

THE TORCH OF THE TESTIMONY

John W. Kennedy tells the little known, almost forgotten, story of evangelical Christians during the dark ages.

CHRISTIAN BOOKS PUBLISHING HOUSE

BOOKS BY GENE EDWARDS

THE DIVINE ROMANCE

The most powerful, arresting book we have ever published. With a might and beauty that sweeps from eternity to eternity, here is, truly, the greatest love story ever told. If you have any interest at all in the deeper Christian life, then, by all means, read this book. Rarely, if ever, has the depth and mystery of Christ been put so simply, yet so profoundly and so breathtakingly beautiful.

A TALE OF THREE KINGS

A book beloved around the world. A dramatically told tale of Saul, David and Absalom, on the subject of brokenness. A book used in the healing of the lives of many Christians who have been devastated by church splits and by injuries suffered at the hands of other Christians.

OUR MISSION

A group of Christian young men in their early twenties met together for a weekend retreat to hear Gene Edwards speak. Unknown to them, they were about to pass through a catastrophic split. These messages were delivered to prepare those young men spiritually for the inevitable disaster facing them. Edwards presents the standard of the first century believers and how those believers walked when passing through similar crises. A remarkable statement on how a Christian is to conduct himself in times of strife, division and crisis. A book every Christian, every minister, every worker will need at one time or another in his life.

INWARD JOURNEY

Crossing time and space, a young man named Chris Young learns the Christian meaning of transformation. A study in suffering, pain and the ways of God in our lives.

LETTERS TO A DEVASTATED CHRISTIAN

Gene Edwards writes a series of letters to a Christian who has been deeply damaged by a crisis in the group he has been part of. A book that has brought help, counsel and healing to many hurt Christians.

If you are just getting acquainted with books on the deeper Christian life, we would like to suggest what may be the best approach to reading books on this subject. There is not a great deal of literature available in this area of the Christian walk, so you will wish to make the most of what is available.

We recommend that you begin your reading with THE DIVINE ROMANCE. Follow with EXPERIENCING THE DEPTHS OF JESUS CHRIST and PRACTICING HIS PRESENCE. THE DIVINE ROMANCE will stir and give insight and prepare you for the practical and spiritual help found in the other two books.

Two other books which complement EXPERIENCING THE DEPTHS OF JESUS CHRIST are UNION WITH GOD and THE SPIRITUAL GUIDE.

You will also find real profit in reading THE SPIRITUAL LETTERS of Jeanne Guyon and THE SPIRITUAL LETTERS of Fenelon. Many of the questions and problems of your daily walk with Christ and your relationship with others are dealt with in these two books.

For insight into brokenness and to see just what the heart of a man of God should be, the beautiful A TALE OF THREE KINGS is a book you will want to read again and again. If you would like to know more about the ways and purposes of the cross, suffering and transformation (which must come into the life of all Christians), then you will want to read THE INWARD JOURNEY.

DIVINE LIFE might be looked upon as a technical explanation of the human spirit and its difference from the human soul, but having read this book, you will be pleased to know more about the spiritual process going on inside you. This book is a great help to Christians in their quest to get a handle on their spirit.

THE EARLY CHURCH, Volume I, the story of the body of Christ from Pentecost to Antioch, will give you insight into what "church life" meant in the first century.

THE TORCH OF THE TESTIMONY tells the story of the church and church life as it survived during the dark ages and beyond.

The following prices are for the year 1985 *only*; please write for our catalog for price update and for new releases.

The Divine Romance (Edwards) . . . . (10.95 hb) 7.95 pb
Experiencing the Depths of Jesus Christ (Guyon) 4.95
The Spiritual Adventure (Guyon) 7.95
Practicing His Presence (Lawrence) 4.95
The Inward Journey (Edwards) 5.95
A Tale of Three Kings (Edwards) 5.95
The Spiritual Guide (Molinos) 5.95
Guyon's Letters 6.95
Fenelon's Letters 5.95
The Early Church (Edwards) 4.95
Torch of the Testimony (Kennedy) 6.95
Our Mission (Edwards) 8.95
Letters to A Devastated Christian (Edwards) 3.95
Guyon's Commentaries:
    Genesis 5.95
    Exodus (The Way Out) 7.95
    Song of Songs 5.95
    Job 7.95
    Revelation (Christ Our Revelation) 8.95
The Biography of Mme. Guyon (Upham) 8.95

CHRISTIAN BOOKS
PUBLISHING HOUSE
Box 959
Gardiner, Maine 04345
207-582-4880
Visa–Mastercard accepted

Christian Books sponsors an Annual Conference on the deeper Christian life each summer in Maine, as well as other week-long conferences in New England. Please write for details.